Soothe Your Soul

Ivor Green

This book is dedicated to family and friends, past and present, whose time in my life has brought to me the experiences I needed to arrive at this place of gratitude.

◆ FriesenPress

Suite 300 – 990 Fort St
Victoria, BC, Canada, V8V 3K2
www.friesenpress.com

Copyright © 2015 by Ivor Green
First Edition – 2015

ivor.sootheyoursoul@gmail.com

The intent of the author is only to offer information of a general nature to help you in your quest for emotional and spiritual well-being. In the event you use any of the information in this book for yourself the author and publisher assume no responsibility for the results of your actions.

All rights reserved. No part of this publication may be reproduced in any form, or by any means, electronic or mechanical, including photocopying, recording, or any information browsing, storage, or retrieval system, without permission in writing from FriesenPress.

ISBN
978-1-4602-7424-8 (Paperback)
978-1-4602-7425-5 (eBook)

1. *Self-Help, Spiritual*
2. *Self-Help, Personal Growth*
3. *Self-Help*

Distributed to the trade by The Ingram Book Company

Table of Contents

Introduction xi

Chapter 1   Oneness and Separation — 1
Our lost connection with Spirit — 1

Chapter 2   The Pain of Separation — 5
Early impressions form our reality — 5
Our learning experience — 7
The influence of those around us — 9
We are all perfect — 12

Chapter 3   Ego — 15
What is ego? — 15
What does ego look like when it shows up? — 17
Ego is active if we feel alone — 17
Ego shows up in regret and self-criticism — 17
Worry is a very effective activity of ego — 18

Ego is active in victim behaviour	18
Addiction is heavily aligned with ego	18
Ego feeds on pain	19
Ego revels in feeling "not good enough"	19
Judgment and criticism are ego-driven	21
Perfectionism is an activity of the ego	22
Ego is not all bad.	22
Ego fights to suppress Spirit	23
Awareness precedes change	24

Chapter 4 The Real You — 25
- Live from the inside out — 27
- Trust the power within — 29

Chapter 5 Now Time — 35
- The present and the small voice within — 35
- How do we get into now time? — 39
- Setting intention — 40

Chapter 6 Energy — 43
- We are energy in motion — 43
- There is hope – lots of hope — 45
- What you resist persists — 46
- Things to watch for — 50
- What not to do with our energy — 51
- The energy you put out pulls in your experience of life — 53

Chapter 7 The Big Cover-up — 55
- What we do to hide from ourselves — 55
- Nobody can make us angry without our permission — 57
- Health issues and addictions — 57
- Trust and abandonment — 59

Attachment to results	60
Anywhere but in the present moment	60

Chapter 8   How We Show Up In Life — 63
A brief compilation of our attributes and challenges — 64

Chapter 9   The Mirror of Life — 71
Are we serving Spirit, or serving an illusion? — 72
How do we know what to change? — 73
Life is a perfect reflection of what is happening inside — 73
Identifying what is in the mirror of life — 80
It is all about you — 85
What to look for — 85
Relationships — 87
Health — 90

Chapter 10   Forgiveness — 93
Explaining the need for forgiveness — 94
Forgiving others, forgiving self — 96
Combining compassion, forgiveness, and love — 97
Affirmations and imaging — 99
Applying the principles involved — 107

Chapter 11   Healing Attitudes — 111
Recognizing Spirit — 112
Faith — 112
Trust and doubt — 113
Feeling — 113
Security — 114
More than I know — 114
High self-regard — 114
Loyalty – honour ourselves — 115

Avoid victim thinking	115
Choice	116
Openness to receive	116
Happiness	116
Freedom	117
Perfection within	118
Performance	118
Health	118
Acceptance	119
Letting go	119
Willingness	119
Success	120
Time	120
The "Challenge."	121
Change	121
What goes around comes around	122
Patience	123
Results	123
A reason, a season, or a lifetime	123
Chapter 12 Action	125
Partnering with Spirit	125
Intention	129
Focus	132
Non-attachment	134
Action	135
Reminders	137
Hazards and roadblocks	142
Chapter 13 Communication	151
Communicate with the inner self first	151
Then communicate with others	152

Chapter 14 **Love**	155
What is love?	155
Aspects of love	158
Relationships	160
Acknowledgements	163
References	165

Introduction

The basic premise of this book is that we are a Spirit housed in a human body having a unique, temporary, human experience.

This book presents an overview of how we stumble through life and what adjustments we can make in order to have more fun on this journey.

The initial chapters involve painting a picture of how we got to where we are and the important things that affect our lives profoundly on a daily basis: the ability to live in now time; how energy flows; the painful baggage we drag with us from the past, and the ego that is constantly tugging at us in an attempt to run our lives.

How we react to life is reviewed in Chapter 7, The Big Cover-up. We unconsciously work hard to cover up those things that are, in effect, holding us back from a more enjoyable life.

What can we do to recover some lost ground and heal ourselves? The life that we are experiencing is a perfect reflection of what is going on inside of us. It is telling us what needs healing. Once armed with an understanding of what we need to heal we can apply compassion, forgiveness, and love to create healing for ourselves – healing that can bring us more in tune with our Spirit and thereby create more joy and happiness in our lives. Some suggestions are provided on attitude and action that can help us stay in balance in our daily living.

Each person's journey is unique. However, the principles involved in our daily lives are similar and the mirror of life can reveal all with precision if we encourage it to happen.

There are theme subjects running through this book that are there because of their significance in the daily lives of so many.

It is my desire that this book will provide some "Aha!" moments that will help make readers happier and wiser through a better understanding of who we are in this seemingly complicated world. As you make life easier you help to *Soothe Your Soul* and have it express more fully into your life.

May you be blessed with love, peace, good health, and happiness.

Namaste

Chapter 1

Oneness and Separation

Our lost connection with Spirit

What is it that I believe? Am I Spirit having a human experience, or a human being trying to have a spiritual experience? If I accept that I am Spirit having a human experience, I can more easily consider the concept of Oneness. I believe that there is a Creator whose Being is beyond our human comprehension. I believe this Being to be a benevolent one who has created the circumstances of our existence. The plants and animals around us come from this same Source.

It is a challenge to describe in words the blissful feeling that goes with the feeling of Oneness, of being at peace with our own Spirit and the Spirits of those around us. When we feel this connection there is a great sense of

peace
love
being present to this moment
outcomes not being important
allowing life to flow
feeling connected

feeling free of the need for anything

We cannot think our way to Oneness; we have to feel our way. We need to experience the feeling of Oneness, to feel this sense of connection, inner peace, love, and joy that is the expression of true inner Spirit.

Each one of us is born of and connects with the One Spirit that is within all of us. We are One, you are me and I am you, living, in part, to understand life's mystery. Yes, we have these wonderful feelings from time to time, but they should represent our normal state of being, not the exception.

We need to acknowledge and embrace this concept of Oneness in order to help ourselves overcome some of the barriers that are preventing us, as a human race, from living in balance and harmony. To have faith that this One Source has benevolent intent in which we can trust is a great asset in our healing journeys.

We are born of Spirit and clothed in our human bodies so that we may have a human experience. For the most part we have lost that sense of connection with Spirit and live out our daily lives in a disconnected state.

As children we have grown through those fragile years exposed to a sense that there is "not enough" or "I am not good enough." Alternatively, many of us have been exposed to the pain of others through verbal or physical abuse, or simply been shown poor examples of how to live. As children we are unable to reason and we may have made some wrong assumptions. As vulnerable children we accepted our circumstances and the sense of separation was underway.

We have become so separate from Spirit that we spend most of our time in a world we have created for ourselves, and consequently cannot recognize Spirit within others or ourselves. We have created a whole outer world with its own set of values and concepts about life.

The end of our lifetime brings the question of "death" and many of us live in fear of this moment for much of our lives. Death is not uppermost in our minds and we simply do not want to contemplate death. And even though we hold an underlying fear of death, many religions talk of an afterlife.

If there is "life" after "death" then how final is death? If we are Spirit, and Spirit lives on, then what has died? It is just our bodies that have expired. We have come to accept the physical being to be the person we know, and this is an example of our sense of separation. When we lose someone we feel a huge sense of physical loss, and we are certainly going to miss his or her presence in our lives, but that person's Spirit has not died. At some funerals this transition is treated with a celebration. People don't die. Their bodies perish like flowers at the end of summer, but they are perennials by virtue of being Spirit, ready to be reborn.

We further our sense of separation by giving this Creator names that create the impression we are all separate entities. In fact, we are an extension of our Creator, a Creator in which we need to trust, for without that trust our Creator cannot help us. We may ask our Creator to intervene but at the same time there is something we must remember. In order to give us responsibility for our lives our Creator cannot interfere with our choices. Our Creator and our own Spirit are silent partners working on our behalf for our better good. The only thing that is preventing their success is the interference that we are running through the sense of separation.

If you have this book in your hands, you are seeking. In this book I would like to explore the possibilities for letting go of our "outer world" in order to align ourselves closer to the Spirit that we are within, our connection to Oneness. A few of us make this transition rapidly but for most of us it is a gradual process.

There is tremendous power at our disposal if we would but tap into that power. The choice is ours to seek it. The energy of our searching will bring us glimpses of encouragement, leaving us to persevere so that we spend more time in this space.

The greeting "Namaste" goes back centuries and has different meanings in different cultures. I close this chapter with a beautiful definition of the greeting Namaste that came to me via e-mail, author unknown.

"Namasté – I honour the place in you in which the entire Universe dwells. I honour the place in you, which is love, of truth, of light, and of peace. When you are in that place in you, and I am in that place in me, we are One."

May your journey to Oneness be blessed with success.

Chapter 2

The Pain of Separation

The greater part of human pain is unnecessary. It is self-created as long as the unobserved mind runs your life"

– Eckhart Tolle, A New Earth

Early impressions form our reality

The separation from Spirit starts before we are born. Spirit enters the womb to take on a human form in order to experience life from the perspective of another dimension. The foetus senses the positive and negative energy of the people outside the womb and the journey of separation begins.

Once we are born, the separation process gathers speed. The experts say that at least half of our development occurs in the first two years of life. Unfortunately, this all occurs when we lack the ability to apply reason to the events happening around us. By the age of seven most of our major impressions of life have already been formed. This occurs before we have a chance to realise that we are Spirit having a human experience.

Consequently, our human experience becomes what we observe. All the information received comes from outside of us, and, not surprisingly, we come to believe that life is "out there." We have not had the opportunity to consciously recognise our true inner Spirit and the outside world becomes all important. Our world involves interaction with those around us and we develop our personalities based on that feedback.

Our inner persona develops based upon what we observe and learn. This inner persona is known only to us, albeit unconsciously. It is built around our belief system that in turn is based on outside experiences. This inner persona is our private world and is the basis of the ego.

Our persona expresses itself to others in our daily lives as our personalities. Our personalities are not necessarily a true representation of how we feel inside as ego seeks to manipulate outcomes and we endeavour to conform to societies expectations.

The story is often told of the sadness behind the mask of the clown who creates laughter. In a like manner, we put on a brave face to the world so that no one else can see what we do not wish to confront about ourselves, or that we do not want others to see about us. This conflict adds to life's difficulty.

Some of what we learn serves us well in our daily lives, and some of what we learn appears to make our life more challenging. All experiences, whether they are observed to be positive or negative in their influence on our lives, will eventually serve us in a positive way. This might not be obvious at first, but in time both positive and negative experiences offer an opportunity for us to see that they have had added benefits to us in our journey.

There are many influences at home – parents, siblings, foster parents, stepparents, stepbrothers and sisters, and other family members may be living with us. All of them will give us viewpoints on life and experiences that will cause us to form opinions about how life is from our point of view. That point of view becomes deeply embedded and we represent it as who we are.

We have observed what is going on around us; we have noticed what is being said to us and what actions are being done toward us. Unconsciously, we have made judgments about all of these interactions. We have integrated this into who we think we are and begin experiencing life from this point of view as we move into adulthood.

Our learning experience

The experiences of the younger years are so important and create the beliefs on which our life is based. What happens in the home is vital. Was it a happy home where there were lots of smiles and laughter, or was there mostly bickering and fighting? The overall feeling of the home is so important and creates the perception of love that is carried forward into life. A happy home will create a sense that the world is safe; an unhappy home will create fear in the young child and the belief that the world is not a safe place in which to live.

Some of the basic truths that follow will sound familiar, perhaps because they reflect common wisdom:

If there is love in the household the adult will find love in the world.

If the child is treated with fairness the adult will care about others.

If they feel shame in a household there will be a sense of guilt.

If the child experiences criticism she/he will learn to criticize others in the unconscious hope that making them feel less important will bring feelings of higher self-importance.

Violence replicates as violence.

Encouragement brings on confidence.

Arguing adults in a home create a sense of hostility.

Witnessing parents working through their differences with good communication will cause the adult to meet life with positive expectancy.

Observing tolerance will help one to move through life with patience.

When raised by a perfectionist the inclination will be to put a rod to our own back as we try to emulate them.

Gentleness leads to compassion.

Living in poverty creates a sense of "never having enough."

Experiencing rejection and criticism results in a feeling of "not being good enough."

When we do not feel there is enough we worry about having enough in the future, a condition that undermines physical health.

Being constantly berated will lead to withdrawal.

Being unfairly treated will eventually cause resentment.

Being told we are "not good enough" will lead to procrastination and avoiding success so that we continue to feel "not good enough."

Discipline provides boundaries; without them we become vulnerable to other peoples' points of view.

Hearing people say one thing and do another leads to cynicism.

If enough things are perceived to be going against us then we may well develop a sense of inferiority that will lead to a lack of confidence.

The influence of those around us

The sphere of influence does not stay within the home. Off to school we go to learn what others would have us know. Rules, regulations, and a fixed curriculum prepare us to enter the business world. Are we free to learn as we wish, to question without limitation, to challenge the "system?" Are we taught how to think and to question, or are we taught what to think? We are judged on our performance and our marks are compared to others; we are graded like cattle at a meat market. Often we are not encouraged to think or act freely, to truly form our own opinions. As we mature, some of the limitations are lifted but it is a brave soul that selects this path so soon and walks against the status quo. As adolescents we are challenged with puberty, early relationships, break-ups, a certain amount of cruelty and ridicule toward each other, peer pressure, available drugs, and competition on the sports field where there are more comparisons. Instead of sports being fun we may have endured parents screaming from the sidelines for better performance, perhaps to live out their own unfulfilled dreams.

Perhaps you have been raised in a strongly religious family with more rules, regulations, people, and clergy telling you how to think, how to act, and what to believe about life. Perhaps you have come from another country steeped in traditions and viewpoints very different from those in your new adopted home. Young immigrants must balance the cultural integration between parents and their new peer group.

The above is written on the assumption that both parents were present. Perhaps there were years spent in a foster home. Maybe you were raised by a single parent, which often involves financial hardships. Maybe your upbringing was affected by divorce or the death of a parent. All these scenarios have a huge impact on how a child views the world. The situation of a missing parent can create a lot of emotional distress and generate a lot of anger in an effort to mask the pain.

The subject of a breach of trust warrants special attention. Remember that we are dealing with children's perceptions: how they interpret what is going on around them, what words and events mean to them. A child who feels betrayed has difficulty trusting. In addition to the loss of trust, incest and sexual abuse are devastating to the developing sense of self. This sort of childhood can lead a person into all sorts of activity to cover up the inner pain. Betrayal of trust has the potential for the deepest wounds, and the ones most difficult to heal. It could involve imposing the same abuse on others, promiscuity or addictions to drugs or alcohol. I know from hearing about the personal experiences of others and from reading statistics that far too many people have these kinds of experiences in their background.

Abandonment is another punishing experience that leaves deep wounds. Abandonment can be factual or it can be perceived as abandonment through the eyes of the child. For example, divorce to a child can easily be interpreted as abandonment by one parent, despite all of their efforts relating to parental visitation.

Another way of picking up a sense of pain and separation is by silent assimilation. This is much more difficult to identify in the healing process. A child looks up to the parent and tries to emulate them in every way. We are all energy and our feelings can be transferred from one person to another at a very subtle level, without any actions being visibly directed toward the recipient. Ed's story was of such an experience. He was very angry inside despite being raised in a stable, quiet household. He struggled to cope with his anger, often suppressing his feelings. He could not understand how he came to feel this way until one day he witnessed his father blowing up over nothing. He shared this with his sister and learned she had observed several such outbursts. His sister was also dealing with a huge amount of anger and often expressed angry outbursts.

Ed considered what he knew about his father's very difficult upbringing. He acknowledged that his father was attempting to be a model citizen but could not always hold his unresolved and suppressed feelings in check. He could see where his father's background could lead to deep-seated anger. Ed has spent his childhood in the presence of this angry energy and it had crossed over quietly and invisibly from his father to be part of who he is today.

Having a job is essential for nearly all of us and at some point we are introduced to working for a living. Again, we have competition. We are graded, reviewed, and subjected to other peoples' power trips. We are in an arena with many others, each protecting their pain and acting to cover it up, sometimes at our expense. There is so much going on and it can be so confusing. We do not really know ourselves, so we can hardly expect to understand where someone else is coming from. Does it feel like chaos? Well, it is. And it is up to us to find our balance in all of this.

In adulthood we enter into relationships. Some of the pain being carried by the individual enters the relationship and comes to the surface, but often is not resolved. This lack of resolution drives the pain deeper. If the partners move on with damaged egos and only partial or no resolution, the pattern tends to repeat itself in any new relationship.

Elsie related how she was coming home from school one day at the age of ten when she met her father, whom she loved dearly, walking toward her carrying a suitcase. He said good-bye and left the country. She did not see him again until years later he showed up on Christmas Day, by which time she was the single mother of three children. I cannot imagine how she felt. I do know that based on this, and other painful experiences with men in her childhood, that she had difficulty trusting men. Elsie lived in fear of her partner leaving her.

It is a wonder anyone arrives at the threshold of adulthood with any sort of sanity.

What goes into the child comes out of the adult. As adults we live out what we have learned until we take a good look at what is not serving us. On close scrutiny we will learn that we are "acting out" on the pain that we have learned from other people or events. This is not our pain but it is affecting, if not running, our lives. The pain, through the vibrations of energy, brings challenging events and circumstances into our lives and we become so absorbed in dealing with our reactions that we are unconscious of our own Spirit.

We are all perfect

The longer that we live embracing our persona the more separate we will feel from Spirit. We are living outside of ourselves in a world of separation, which sometimes feels like a world of quiet desperation.

When we end up with too many issues complicating our lives it is difficult to live life with passion. Our zeal for life is gradually worn down. The pain from the past becomes more than memories and we become a prisoner of our own persona. Separation has taken over.

As an adult, life brings us mixed results. Our energy is causing life to replicate what we, in our early years, judged life to be about. This brings us to the opportunity to choose a new reaction to events in our lives.

You and I are One in this world and yet we live in a world of separation and pain. This sense of separation has been passed down from generation to generation. What is holding you back in any aspect of your life – is it someone else's pain that you have absorbed into your sense of being?

Everyone is perfect and whole in every way, except for the hurts of life.

Remember this, come back to this, for this statement is a reminder of how fragile our individual humanity has become. We need to be gentle with each other. We do not know the journey of another and we would be very wise to refrain from judgment, an aspect of humanity that is so damaging.

There is opportunity to learn from any painful situation. We need to be available to receive that understanding, and this comes after we apply compassion, forgiveness, and love to any situation. Just continuing to look at a situation will not necessarily give us an answer. Ask yourself, "What is it that I need to heal here?"

Chapter 3

Ego

Alone, separated from your divine source, you are a skin encapsulated ego living the illusion that you are important and powerful.

– Wayne Dyer, Manifest Your Destiny

What is ego?

Ego is an identity built around our judgment of what has happened in the past and ego seeks to project that identity into the future. Ego is our inner persona operating like a separate being. Ego has found its identity by looking at the surrounding world and forming judgments about our experiences. These judgments form our belief systems and the basis for how we perceive life. Ego works diligently to preserve the perceptions it holds and seeks to promote itself by convincing our mind that what is good for it is good for us. Ego has developed its own definition of self-worth and relentlessly clings to that definition. Ego is a summation of what we have chosen to believe in, and I do not believe that it is all bad. Ego can also contain strong elements of self-worth that serve us well.

Ego creates a sense of self that is separate from our spiritual identity. Ego is our belief system expressing itself and, unknowingly, in whole or in part, we turn over control of our life to this persona. Ego leads us to experiences and our reaction to those experiences speaks to the world as to who we think we are as a person.

Life is a dichotomy, with love at one end of the spectrum and fear at the other end. Ego represents the fear factor. It is the accumulation of our misconceptions about ourselves.

Ego seeks to maintain the status quo in order to carry its identity into the future and seeks to protect itself through control.

This is not who we truly are. We are Spirit, but often Spirit is shut out by our beliefs, by our unconscious support of our ego persona. Everything I write to you, every event in my life, will be screened and interpreted by the ego in an attempt to control the outcome. Ego does not want change. Ego wants us locked into its perception of itself and that perception is based on past events.

Ego operates with conditioned responses whenever we are presented with a set of circumstances. Beliefs acquired in the innocence of childhood are acted out in adulthood and continually reinforced. If you feel emotional about something, then ego is lurking because strong emotional responses signal the presence of the energy projected by the ego. (There are exceptions to this, such as grief.) Strong reaction to any pain associated with a belief moves energy and reinforces that about which we are upset. This strong reaction simultaneously reinforces the ego. Ego's principle way of controlling our reactions is to keep us off balance. The ego operates "out there," so actions done in that direction keep us feeling separate. The ego does not want us aligned with our Spirit as that threatens the existence of ego.

What does ego look like when it shows up?

Ego is active when there is control, confusion, judgment, chaos, drama, painful experiences, anger, resentment, and a sense of not being enough. A classic strategy of the ego is to keep our mind focused on anything but the present moment, focused on the past or the future, but never "now."

Ego is active if we feel alone

The ego thrives when it can keep us out of touch with our Spirit, in a state of separation. This can make us feel alone in the world. We are never alone. We can feel lonely at times, yes, but we are never alone. Our Spirit is always at our side to bring peace and contentment, if we would but be open to the opportunity.

Ego shows up in regret and self-criticism

We cannot change the past. It is ego that takes us back and out of the present. We support ego when we are regularly talking about the past, as if we are trying to drag it into the present. The past is gone and can only live on as a memory in our mind. It has become an illusion. We need to stop criticizing ourselves, seek the wisdom in the experience, and move on.

Worry is a very effective activity of ego

Worrying about the future is totally unproductive. When was the last time worrying solved anything for you? Worry solves nothing. We are creating all sorts of pictures of an imaginary future that will not likely ever turn out as feared. Worry is fear based and disturbs the equilibrium of the body. If anything comes of worry it will likely be a breakdown in health, and that is not productive. There is no upside to worry for body or Spirit.

Ego is active in victim behaviour

The cry of the victim is a very sad and tough place to be; a very separate place. "But he, she, the company, bad luck, or drugs did this to me." Victims feel chastised or put upon, the world is against them. Nothing is working, and whatever is going wrong is someone else's fault. My observation is that a person in victim mode puts up resistance to considering the possibility they have any responsibility for their circumstances or for any change. This resistance focuses their energy away from any need to change and just feeds the ego and makes it stronger. The ego is feeding off the pain and the energy put into feeling pain goes to the ego and it grows in stature.

Addiction is heavily aligned with ego

Addictions go beyond drugs and alcohol. One can be addicted to work, a person, to food or chocolate, gambling, sports. An addiction can be represented by any activity that takes up an inordinate amount of time or that leads to manipulation of people and circumstances in order that the addict can continue the behaviour that helps mask their pain.

Ego feeds on pain

It is not enough to burn up their own energy; people in pain will also draw energy from those around them. There may be an inner knowing of what is really happening, which makes them feel worse; they feel guilty and so they have more pain to mask. This is an unenviable downward spiral. Their power feels very much outside of them and puts them, for the time being, beyond effective healing.

Ego seeks to support pain and therefore being happy is not in alignment with its objective. Happiness is a state of Be-ing. It is not found outside of us and does not come from outside sources, such as from the acquisition of a new possession or entering into a new relationship. Buddhist philosophy believes all unhappiness comes from self-centredness. We are too often looking for happiness and thereby support our ego. We have to move into the present moment to be happy.

Ego revels in feeling "not good enough"

In *A New Earth*, Eckhart Tolle comments, *"Why does the ego play roles? Because of one unexamined assumption, one fundamental error, one unconscious thought. That thought is: "I am not enough."*

Pain from old experiences is carried forward in the form of the ego with a feeling of not being good enough. This feeling can manifest in many ways. Procrastination is but one – it speaks to how we feel about ourselves, our sense of self-worth, and this serves the ego well. Procrastination inevitably denies success and leaves us feeling disappointed and, therefore, not good enough.

I was a talented tennis player when I was young but would shy away from success because somewhere deep inside I did not think I was good enough. I would sometimes get ahead in a match I was not expected to win, and then, when the possibility of winning hit me, I would tighten up and lose. Some feeling inside was telling me I was not good enough to beat my opponent.

Another way ego promotes this feeling is the use of comparisons, such as many we experienced as we grew up. Have you gone past your parents' achievements? This might be difficult to compare, as your parents had different choices in a different time. Can you compare attitudes? Do you feel you have the potential to do more with your life or have you accepted that to reach their level of expectation is sufficient for you? We have more opportunities today. It is okay to outshine our parents. (Most parents would like us to do just that.) This is not about material success, this is about how we celebrate life, how we find and express our passion, how we conduct ourselves as human beings. We compare ourselves to others around us and sometimes even to strangers in the form of celebrities. Is there some fear of comparison holding you back?

The fear of being discovered as not good enough leads to all sorts of action to cover up. When we do not feel good enough we either roll over easily or we strive to prove something. The associated fear kills passion. Our passion is waiting to be discovered, but it is masked. Healing the ego lets Spirit in, and Spirit brings light into our lives, and passion then surfaces.

When we question whether we lack the confidence, talent, resources, knowledge or money, etc. to do something we are suggesting to ourselves that we are lacking. Either we do not feel good enough or we do not feel we have enough to tackle the task at hand. Ego revels in "not enough" or not feeling good enough.

Judgment and criticism are ego-driven

The ego loves to be right and being right feeds the ego's sense of importance. Of course, in order to be right the ego has to identify someone as wrong. To put someone else down is tantamount to a judgment. This leads to being self-righteous and eventually to being angry in defence of our ego position. We place our perfect ego sense onto others and get angry when they do not live up to our ideals. Do you ever justify your position? Do you ever catch yourself being defensive? What are you defending? What is it about yourself that leaves you feeling uncomfortable?

Now this is not to be confused with open discussion. We can agree to disagree, but if we are not okay with leaving others with their point of view, then I suggest we are defending an ego driven position. We do not have to convince another person we are right. They have their own viewpoint and their own ego to defend. Would you think some arguments might follow? The alternative is to run away inside and live quietly with our fear. We often avoid confrontation lest we are "exposed."

Perfectionism is an activity of the ego

When we try to be perfect we have to ask what perceived deficiency are we covering for? Our outer projection of ourselves speaks to what is going on inside. We seek to protect the emptiness that is felt inside. In projecting perfectionism our feeling inside is saying we feel less than perfect.

Ego is not all bad.

A gloomy picture has been painted of the ego and most things I have read about ego are negative. However, just as we have developed beliefs that do not serve us well, we also have developed beliefs that have a positive effect on our lives. Both aspects have their roots in what we have observed as we grew up. A simple example is a good work ethic. If we have seen it in our parents as we were growing up we will likely repeat it in our own lives and that then gives us a better chance of earning a living. Consequently, many people function very well in life. They have been shown a good example of how to live. Life comes easier because they expect it to be that way and they have useful tools with which to cope with life, and yet they can still be out of touch with Spirit. They just find it easier to function in this world than others. However, even these people could improve their experience of life if they aligned themselves with Spirit and hence their source of Be-ing.

Ego fights to suppress Spirit

The ego seeks to protect its identity through controlling our actions and reactions. It will influence our outer personality in order to mask its identity, and hence any challenge, from the view of other people.

Like computers, we create our own program as we move up through life based on our beliefs. It has a password – ego – and unless we go past the password, we struggle with the program, and so the program keeps repeating. Getting upset because nothing changes just reinforces the issue. "Wanting" change just reinforces the sense of lack of change. The more energy we focus on what is going wrong in our lives the greater the problem we create. Ego feeds on itself and with time wears us down into submission. It is our choice to change. New beliefs conflict with old beliefs and are a major challenge to ego if we choose to change; the change is our choice and ours alone to make.

Is your life full of dramas, large or small? Is there lots of "stuff" happening that gives you lots to react to and talk about? There are no accidents. "Stuff" is happening to keep us focused away from this moment. Ironically, the ego provides us with all the pointers we need to identify what needs to be healed by regularly bringing our attention to what is not going well in our lives. Our part is to be alert to what is going on – the key observations and clues are that we are not always enjoying our feelings or circumstances.

The focus of the ego will draw in circumstances for us to work through, and if we resist our energy passes to what we resist and it grows, and so does the challenge we are resisting. Ego grows right along with it. When we are feeling down and out we are likely resisting change desired by Spirit.

Awareness precedes change

Life appears as a three-way battle between Spirit (represented by love), ego (represented by fear), and other peoples' pain. Release the latter two and we receive what is left, the love that flows with being in touch with Spirit.

First, there is nothing proactive to do about the ego. Life is a matter of letting go of the ego beliefs about who we think we are. In order to experience a state of Oneness the activity of the ego has to be silenced. That process starts by bringing things into awareness, and as we look at our beliefs they dissolve and we are one step closer to identifying with Spirit.

I have maintained for many years that one of the greatest shortcomings of mankind is our ability to think. If we could only feel from our Spirit then life would flow with greater ease. However, the power of thought is also the starting point for change. Ego will do everything possible to pull us away from this moment lest it lose control. It does this by filling our mind with stuff about the past and concern for the outcome of things in the future. This all happens automatically.

Change is possible when we bring something into awareness, into our current "now moment" using our thought process. Thought leads to change. The now moment is our point of power. The thought we are having right now controls our future. If we choose the present moment we could potentially change our view of ourselves and hence change our ego's status.

The options for change are explored more fully later.

Chapter 4

The Real You

If you start to think the problem is "out there," stop yourself. That thought is the problem.

– Stephen Covey, The 7 Habits of Highly Effective People

The problems we face today are created by our belief that we're separate from our Source and each other, leading us to be in a state of conflict. Spirit is who we are, but we express through mind, body, and actions. The difference is whether we are expressing through the power of Spirit or the ego. Which is feeding our actions? We need to understand the difference and have the ability to adapt.

The Real You does not look back at you from the mirror. What you see in the mirror is your body, your means of transportation in this world. Your body is the home in which your Spirit dwells and through which it seeks to express into the world. Spirit is connected to the Oneness of our Creator, the ever-present Power of the Universe. In essence Spirit is invisible, relative to our humanity. Spirit seeks an opportunity to express in our human reality so that it may experience itself on another level. Spirit is like a seed full of the knowledge necessary to form a tree or a plant. However, until that seed takes full physical form it cannot experience the wind blowing between the leaves. In a similar manner, Spirit needs to take on a human body for physical and emotional experiences it cannot have whilst in purely spiritual form. We need to understand that our true essence is this Spirit and that we need to open up to its presence within us and allow it to express. Spirit is not only wise, it is connected to the Power of the Universe; it has infinite possibilities, possibilities beyond our comprehension. We cannot hope to begin to understand those possibilities if we do not allow Spirit to flow. Our life is about Spirit expressing, not the expression of our ego-driven humanity. The potential is ours to embrace – it's free, and all we have to do is be open and willing to embrace Spirit and to let go of those beliefs that block the flow of the river of life.

Here is a special story, a Cherokee Legend.

Two Wolves

One evening an old Cherokee told his grandson about a battle that goes on inside people. He said, "My son, the battle is between two "wolves" inside us all.

One is Evil. It is anger, envy, jealousy, sorrow, regret, greed, arrogance, self-pity, guilt, resentment, inferiority, lies, false pride, superiority, and ego.

The other is Good. It is joy, peace, love, hope, serenity, humility, kindness, benevolence, empathy, generosity, truth, compassion, and faith."

The grandson thought about it for a minute and then asked his grandfather: "Which wolf wins?"

The old Cherokee replied simply, "The one you feed."

Live from the inside out

Our Spirit is our perfection, the source of love, peace, joy, and abundance. We have in many ways discarded this possibility, choosing instead to believe in an outer world. We are living the wrong way around. Instead of living from the inside out, we are living from the outside in. Our outer world is a based on our beliefs. The love and other blessings that flow from Spirit are permanent; they are always present and available. We deny them and choose to believe in what we have created around us, or in our personal beliefs. Our creation is temporary. Spirit lives on. We can reach, touch, and feel things around us, and for sure they feel real. They are certainly a part of our lives, but they are not who we are. The true reality is we are Spirit and that is the one reality. Love is all there is, the rest is illusion.

What we have created around us is just that – a creation. If we can see that creation for what it is, all is well. If we believe it is part of who we are, or feel we need it to exist, we have aligned ourselves with an illusion. It is illusion because we have created its importance by our attitude toward that on which we are focused. When we change our focus the importance changes. Something that can be forever changing is not real – it can perish in an instant. It is our creation, so we can change our attitude and the value that we have given to the things and people around us.

We strive to be "perfect" in our human world, a view skewed by an ego that has a status quo to maintain. We already are perfection and do not have to look elsewhere or achieve anything in order to prove it. Each of us is perfection, as perfect as the Spirit that we truly are. It is a different type of perfection from that which our ego might pursue.

There is abundance and we should want for nothing. However, we, in our humanity, continue to want for so much, which is brought about by our own denial of who we truly are. We are feeding our egos instead of allowing Spirit to flow. It is time to separate from the beliefs and vibrations we have assumed and then we will automatically pull back the veil and discover Spirit. This is hard to envision because we have fought to keep Spirit out. Consequently, our experience of Spirit is limited, or, in some cases, non-existent.

Once again I say we need to live from the inside out, not the outside in. We cannot place reliance for our joy and well-being on anything "out there." It is all a creation, temporary and subject to moving out of our lives. We cannot align our sense of identity with another person, a relationship, an achievement, or any possession. They are important to us, they are part of our life, but they are no substitute for whom we truly are within.

We have been blessed with incredible choice. Our Source has provided this blessing and has put us in charge, to do with as we wish. Our Source has granted us responsibility. We cannot grant someone responsibility and then look over their shoulder and tell them how to do something. In so doing we have taken back the responsibility. A former manager of mine once said to me, "I won't interfere in what you are doing, or I cannot hold you responsible when you screw up and I want to fire you." He was so right, and I found his attitude very liberating.

So we are the managers of this blessing and looking around me it is obvious that we are not doing well. There are some remarkable people striving to keep us together against significant odds. It is time for us all to step up to the plate, take charge of our own lives and subsequently make a more meaningful contribution to this planet and help it to heal through the power of love.

Trust the power within

It is time to separate from ego and stand in our perfection, to experience trust in our Source. To know that there is abundance for not just you and me, but for everyone. When we trust we have no fear. We believe in living a great today, and then tomorrow will follow in like manner. What we experience today is an expression of what we projected into the Universe in our yesterdays. Today well lived makes tomorrow a vision of hope. Our disappointments can only lie in our denial of who we truly are, in our belief in fear over love, putting ego above Spirit.

It is a challenge to suddenly switch over and trust in something we cannot see. We have experienced so many examples of a breach of trust, both individually and collectively. Governments act with dishonour. In business we are bombarded with requests to shade our integrity. This does not mean we have to do something, we may just be asked to stay silent, against our better judgement. Remember, omission to act is a choice and an "act" in itself. It is hard to step out against such injustice when we perceive our paycheque is on the line. In these situations we are truly inside the "system." Omissions to act or speak up are equal errors to when we do something in error. Turning our lives over to Spirit is much like stepping off a cliff blindfolded on someone's guarantee that there is a safety net there to catch us.

We are beings of incredible possibility. Trusting the inside instead of what is visible around us is a huge choice. Trust is a core issue for humanity, let alone for us individually. The subject is in our face constantly – just check the news. We are now telling our children more than ever not to trust strangers. Now we are learning they cannot trust all of their trustees outside of family – coaches, ministers, youth leaders, etc. There are just a few "rotten apples" in the barrel that change our attitudes and make it difficult for the sincere majority trying to make a positive difference. Sad to say, most trust issues still emanate from family members. Lack of trust looks ugly, and, like everything else, it will only change by moving forward one step at a time. We have to take those steps in our own lives in order to make our contribution to the whole, to raise the energy and well-being on this planet.

We have that power within. "Ask and ye shall receive" is not an idle statement. We are born with power, the same power as anyone else – that is what is meant by being born equal. If we have the faculties to read this book then we have the ability to express that power. Not all of us are in a position to recognize the choice. Believe in abundance; it is okay to receive. When we ask, don't hold out a thimble to receive, for then a thimbleful is all we can collect.

This is all about you, the power within, about taking charge, trusting, and finally giving. This is a life about giving and sharing the best of us and not about getting or accumulating. Life is not about achievements, but rather, about what we are after we have the education or the success we seek. Once we have attained something in this society how do we then give back?

It is time to step out of fear. Do we fight fear? No! Fight nothing; embrace everything. To fight against anything is to give energy to that which we oppose and it must then grow. We must step forward with our own agenda, our own vision and our own intention. Act *for* something, never against it. For example, although the organization Mothers Against Drunk Driving have worked wonders, they might have done even better if they were Mothers *for* Sober Driving. Which vision are the words creating? Our minds bring up a vision after reading the words to which our energy flows. Which vision is the more positive, drunk driving or sober driving?

This book suggests we heal those events around us in an effort to clear the way to connecting with Spirit. However, when all is said and done, it is all about you. It does not matter what others think – what do you think about yourself when you look in the mirror? Are you happy with what you observe? Life is an opportunity to express, to experience, to be closer to Spirit than ego, to express Spirit before ego and know the difference.

In order to overcome the ego I assure myself that I am okay as I am. I am okay on my own because I am never on my own. We are all One and the Source is with us every moment of the day and night.

The ultimate goal is the unwavering belief that we are Spirit and to feel that Spirit coming through in every "now moment." Keep attention on self, honour self; life is about self, so ensoul the positives we choose. Life is an inside job;

focus on giving and not seeking to receive. Just be open to receive. Remember that you are worthy to receive.

It is our humanity that has got in the way by holding on to the old patterns and ego concepts. When you choose to move toward enlightenment you bring things into awareness, with acceptance and without judgment. A Spiritual person never judges, they just observe what is, in that moment. Step back and be the observer of your mind and then take charge, become the director of your life and move toward your intention.

We need to stop trying to create a sense of importance. We are already important and need only lead a life of intention from that self-acceptance of who we are. As with everything, we are already there – we are important but possibly, probably, in denial. Once we separate ourselves from the vibrations of our humanity, of ego, then we are free to discover Spirit.

So what does it feel like to be in Spirit? Awesome! What do we look like? No different than how we are now, other than maybe our faces will look softer, more relaxed, and our eyes brighter. It is a state of peace within, of living without fear, of being in the moment and understanding its power, meaning, and importance, living a life of unconditional love, living without judgement, embracing acceptance and being forever grateful. Living in Spirit is to know that on a gloomy day the sun is shining on the other side of the cloud just waiting to shine again on our world, knowing that this moment too will pass and reveal its wisdom.

Remember to squeeze the juice out of life, every moment, every meeting, the sight of every flower and the sound of every song. Remember your power comes from your Source; trust in it and its wonderful benevolence, a benevolence that is only blocked out by your human fears and ego. In order to make a difference, sometimes we need to get close to and be surrounded by the less than perfect energy of others. It calls for awareness, an awakening. Hence the feeling that the world is crazy – it is!

You are number one in your world, in every aspect of your life. Nobody makes your heart beat, nobody can do this for you. Your heart beats for you, you sleep, eat, and function for you. Nobody can do anything for you that only you can do for yourself.

Love yourself. But then who are you? You have to decide who you are so you can love the concept of who you are – you are not the physical body in the mirror, but love your body anyway. Your body houses your Spirit and is its avenue of expression.

It all comes down to our relationship with ourselves. How are we doing, are we enjoying life with its current results?

Be humble. I seek to be more than I believe I am, and yet if I let go of this outer perception I will discover that I am more than I could have imagined.

It is time now to explore some of the factors that are important when we contemplate life and change.

Chapter 5

Now Time

Whatever the present moment contains, accept it as if you had chosen it. Always work with it, not against it. Make it your friend and ally, not your enemy. This will miraculously transform your whole life.

– Eckhart Tolle, The Power of Now

The present and the small voice within

In order to be in "now time" it is necessary to be fully present in this moment, not concerned with what was happening five minutes ago or will be happening five minutes hence.

Now – right now!

Life only exists in the present moment. The future is not happening now and neither is the past – they are both just places where our mind likes to take us. Both are non-existent.

The past is done. The future is another present moment waiting to happen. The present moment is the "present," a gift from the Source of our Be-ing. The present moment is the gift of life itself. The present moment is really all there is. It is the only moment in which life can be lived. To be anywhere else is a mind game. We are in trouble because we do not know how to stop thinking.

This is why "now time," the present moment, is so important. It is the point of power. It aligns with Spirit, for "now time" is the only "time" that Spirit knows. Spirit makes its powerful connection with us in this moment. It cannot help at any other time because any other time reference is an illusion, an activity of the mind. Such an illusion is a time that does not exist.

It is in now time that it is possible to harness the loving energy of Spirit. In now time there is no wasted time, because we are staying away from past and future. The past is a resource, a library of experience from which to draw. The future is not to be ignored. A plan of intention gives a framework from which to base decisions in this moment to move toward our intention for the future, toward manifestation. By staying in now time Spirit is at our side and Spirit can guide us along the most beneficial route to secure our intention. By staying focused, Spirit is embraced and it provides guidance toward the best solution available. The "present" of now time is a most powerful gift. It helps us step out of the turmoil of time and observe, to be calm, to allow Spirit a chance to come to us in that calm. In the calm of now time we can see clearly, and, more importantly, feel. It is a chance to hear the small voice within.

Life can only be lived now, this moment. How well does society function within this concept? The vast majority spend most of their time away from the present, the gift of life. They live in the past or the future. They are taken there by their minds. And who loves to direct the mind? The ego. It is in the playground of the mind that ego gets a sense of itself succeeding as it endeavours to escape from the interference of Spirit, lest it lose its identity. Spirit is life and can only show up now. If ego can maintain focus on the illusion on either side of this moment, it can carry on creating and securing its identity. The ego has created this sense of time to keep us off balance, for when Spirit flourishes, ego perishes, and that feels like death to the ego. It can feel very uncomfortable when the ego is forced to retreat.

Ego seeks to survive by keeping us separate from the "present" by stealing our gift, our gift of life. The mind is used to direct our life for the initial thought process and ego loves to take over control and direction. And the direction it takes is anywhere but now. Past or future, it matters little to the ego, as long as we are kept separate from the present moment.

We support this concept by dwelling on past events, by allowing the pain of previous experiences to live on as distractions, and worrying about the future and what other people are thinking or what they may expect. Ego focuses attention anywhere but where life exists, anywhere but now. People are, by necessity, busy with the basic activities of daily life. However, do we give ourselves time to tune in to living fully through Spirit? There are lots of potential distractions, such as working overtime or thinking about work when not there. Does family take up so much time there is none left over? Some people are wrapped up in pastimes like photography, sports, or are spending hours in front of a television "killing" time. There is a value in pastimes, but when they take up an excessive amount of time then maybe we should question the ego's motives.

There is so much we do to avoid being "in the moment." Such activity is all a sign that we either do not yet understand the process of life, or we are lost in distractions so that we do not have to consider the challenges that go with being in "now time." There is a false sense of security in these distractions. These are what we know and we cling to our life style rather than step into uncharted territory. The underlying threat is we would have to look at the pain we are suppressing, a potentially scary prospect. We are afraid to relive that pain in order to heal, and therefore we make no progress.

I can only be the in this moment. I cannot do more with my life than I am doing right now. I can only be what I am right now; I can only have intention for future "now moments." The only way is to focus on what is in front of me right now. That may indeed involve using the mind. Practical things do need to be planned, but let Spirit in during those moments. Spirit can still be the guide to the best implementation. Listen for the small voice within. That small voice is not to be heard between the ears, where we are used to listening.

If the voice we can hear can be followed by the mind, I doubt whether it is Spirit coming through – that would be ego. The small voice is hard to describe. I feel Spirit more as a flash of inspiration, a complete thought process delivered in an instant, instinctive, intuitive, but not a thought lumbering along at the speed of the mind. We have all had intuitive moments. Sometimes we ignore them and recall them later when we realize we have made a decision that does not reflect the desire of Spirit. Remember what that moment felt like and stay alert for more. That feeling could be different for each of us. I don't know how it might feel for others – we all have our own receiving system.

How do we get into now time?

Quiet the buzz of life and seek quiet time. For those who live with others this is not always easy. The determined person will find time. Being good to oneself is a discipline. Quiet time is an open act of love toward oneself. Whenever the mind is quiet it opens a peaceful window through which Spirit can communicate. Just focus on something other than what is on the mind, the song of a bird, the steady breathing of your lungs, the wind. Do anything to stop the mind chatter. Stop the mind chatter and ego rests and Spirit rejoices.

Dov Barron asks three simple questions in his workshop in order to get into focus on the moment.

What time is it?

Where am I?

What am I doing?

Meditation is a popular way to quieten the mind and there are many types of meditation and many books on the subject to explore. One objective of meditation is to stop the mind chatter.

Now time is the time to be, without time in mind, just be, quietly focused, loving of self and others. Be in the now, have "now moments," continuously, one after the other.

Living in the now moment is a key to maintaining a loving presence. There is a need to forget about why things are the way they are, this is irrelevant for this exercise. Just notice how they are now. Don't analyse, just watch. We need to observe ourselves, step outside of ourselves and look from the outside, and then decide if we like where we are at in this moment. Then we can consider if we are proud of what we are doing? What would the outcome look like if everyone in the world behaved the same way as we are right now? These are tools to bring us into the moment.

Once we are in that moment we realize that life is about us, the individual. No one else can live our life for us although some may try. And here is something to contemplate, once in that moment: never compromise. Once we compromise ourselves we are on the slippery slope to resentment. Cooperate by all means, but never compromise. Once you have declared to yourself who your life is really about you invoke Spirit.

Accept what is happening in this moment; in fact, embrace it. Resistance will only grow that which we do not like. Bring the happening into the awareness of now and see it for what it is, an opportunity.

Setting intention

Focus on this moment and this one only. When we slow down and disconnect from time we are be able to accomplish more, as our concentration is not scattered. Focus on something, get right into it, and notice how much you get accomplished because you are in the moment for a long time. Time "flies" when we are not "in the moment," for every moment we are out of now time we are not living, and so the "present" moments of life itself pass us by. Remember – a "now moment" is the "present" of life.

Now that you have arrived in this moment, at your point of power, put vitality into this moment; the vitality will radiate out as a powerful energy, for this is the most powerful moment. This is the moment in which to truly create. Then follow up and do your best to stay in "now time."

We do need a plan for where we are going, but not one held so rigidly that Spirit cannot guide. Have your intention set for when you arrive at that point, that now moment that lies in the future. That way, when we arrive at that moment, we will be better prepared to respond to the circumstances of that moment. A ship without a rudder will follow the current, even if it is heading for the big drop of Niagara Falls.

Chapter 6

Energy

Energy flows to where the concentration goes.

We are energy in motion

Spirit is not visible; it is energy, just as our thoughts are energy. In this chapter I would like to reflect on energy and how it flows in our lives.

We are energy in motion and energy is constantly moving around us. Scientists tell us that our "solid" rocks are not so solid, because atoms that compose the rocks are forever in motion. Nothing is standing still. We are held in place by an energy field, otherwise we fall to the floor.

One principle of energy is that it flows to where the concentration goes; a second is that what we concentrate on will expand as the flow of energy builds. These two principles together can raise all sorts of possibilities. I have experienced these principles enough to know they work. When we gain mastery over where our energy is flowing then we will have mastery over how our life goes forward every moment. This is a key aspect of life; I suggest you read this short paragraph over again, it is that important. We are not cognizant of how powerful we are when our Source and our Spirit support us in our choices.

Consider that thought is energy and once created that thought never perishes. The energy associated with that thought can eventually create matter. Therefore, the more that we think about something, the more energy we give to that thought, so we will eventually create circumstances that support our thinking. Our thoughts, everyone one of them, contribute to a result. The result might not be observable immediately; conflicting thoughts may create a stalemate, which is a creation in itself. So we need to be very careful what we think.

We have been granted freedom of choice and our Source will support us in all our decisions. Think of our Source as a big copying machine cranking out copies commensurate with the energy expended by us. And those copies are piling up on our doorstep as per our instructions in the form of life experiences, pleasant or otherwise.

I believe we have been born into a world of abundance but the world does not reflect that back to us. We have widespread poverty and suffering around the world. There is plenty to go around. The problem is just that those that have don't believe they have enough so they are hoarding instead of trusting the flow of abundance. We need to heal individually so that we can enthusiastically support the bigger world picture.

Many of us have a belief there is "not enough," so as we support that concept we resist abundance and what we resist persists. The same problems and healing principles keep surfacing. They do so because they are key elements and very important to understand and act on. So when our underlying, core thought is scarcity, we attract that very experience to ourselves. These repeated experiences come in order for us to understand the error of our thinking.

There is hope – lots of hope

The energy that flows through us from our Source is our opportunity to shine light on our personal world and be a guiding light for others. We stamp that energy with our intention so it is vital that we know what our intention is, that we have boundaries, that we use our energy for giving and not just for getting.

Our life experiences are food for our soul and our Spirit will guide us to those experiences that are needed to nourish us. We have been given the power of choice so we can run a lot of interference for our Spirit. The other option is to co-operate with Spirit and understand how we can best experience life through giving direction to our energy. We can either go with the flow or jump in the water and try swimming upstream. The latter is hard work. When life feels like hard work it is time to check in with ourselves, re-direct our energy and align with a better intention. There is one if we can tune in.

When we are stuck in fear Spirit cannot help us. It comes down to having faith, not in our abilities, but in our Spirit and knowing that only by fearlessly moving forward will we find out what doors Spirit can open for us when we allow the energy to flow positively through us. Energy cannot flow positively when wrapped in fear. Fear is the world of ego.

We are like a radio tuned into a frequency, and this begs the question, to which station are we tuned? In a thunderstorm we get static on the airwaves and poor reception. I liken that to the interference that ego is running in our lives. How well tuned in are you to Spirit?

The radio is tuned in to a station with other like minded people, and so it is in life. We tune in to other like-minded people, as in the saying "birds of a feather flock together." Now there is the corollary of that – "opposites attract." How do both work? Opposites are people working on the same issue, they are just working on it from opposite ends of the spectrum, and so they do have something in common. An example would be a dominant, controlling person hooked up with a submissive person. We attract people into our lives in order to draw our attention to those things we need to heal in order to continue along our journey, be they "birds of a feather" or "opposites" – all situations work to serve a purpose.

What you resist persists

The situation happening right now exists because we have focused on something and given it our energy and the object of our attention expands. For example, many people say they do not have enough money, so where is the energy going, what is getting bigger? – the fact that they do not have enough money. How do they compound this situation? When the paycheque comes in the first thing they pay is the rent or mortgage, then the utilities and other bills, they naturally buy food and who is the last to get paid? Think about it. The first principle in any financial seminar I have been to is "Pay yourself first." What we focus on grows. If our first focus is bills then they will grow; if it is paying ourselves, then our prosperity will grow. It is not that we have to pay ourselves a lot; just put ourselves first on the list instead of last. Recognise yourself and your importance to yourself by putting yourself first. Some readers will challenge this concept on the basis that there are only a finite number of dollars in a paycheque to go around and the order of payment is irrelevant. I agree with the financial speakers and wholeheartedly maintain that the order of payment is very important. Try this concept. The income is still fixed, but somehow it stretches further when approached this way.

Money is a very practical subject to use as a testing ground for where we are spiritually. For many people money is also an emotionally charged subject. Bless your bills and your ability to pay them. Give thanks for the electricity, the heat, the air conditioning, and the services that your taxes provide. Better still; put them all on automatic payment. That way your bills are not in your face every month. They are paid automatically. Automatic payment is a great approach if you are struggling with your attitude toward bills. One of the most damaging thoughts that you can have is thinking about whether you "have enough." Some people, however, have difficulty as money managers and do need a practical approach and set up a monthly budget. Ultimately, all money management has its base in our attitude, in how we are flowing our energy. If we do not believe we have enough, where is the energy flowing, what thought is expanding?

Maybe we say, "I want more money." but it does not come. And that is because want is another word for lack. Reconsider that thought. "I lack more money." Now what is coming off the copying machine? More opportunities to experience the lack of money! I have used money as an example because it is a common issue and one with which most people can relate. The energy concepts presented so far apply not just to money but also to every aspect of our lives, tangible or intangible.

Energy management is a vital part of our lives. We are energy and so is everything around us. As our feelings, thoughts and e-motions flow, so do the results in our lives. There is another old saying that is full of truth: "What goes around comes around." What we give out comes back to us sevenfold, or tenfold, depending on where we read it. The key is about what we focus on – it magnifies. We are back to the copying machine again. What we give out will come back and it will magnify. This is something of which to be aware. Giving in anticipation of receiving will not create the results wished for because that approach is an attempt at manipulation. The underlying thought acknowledges that something is missing, which speaks to lack and so guess what comes back? Whatever we think is missing in our life will remain missing. In order for this approach to work, we have to let go of any attachment to the outcome. Giving means just that, having no anticipation of receiving a reward for your generosity, which of course is not so generous if you are seeking a return. Life is about love and giving is a part of love. It is time to trust in the process of life, to trust in Spirit, in the Source of our creation.

If we have misgivings going on about trust in our lives this whole process is going to stall. We cannot say I trust my Source but not men or women or organisations. We either trust or we don't. We may observe that an individual or organization is unreliable and it is wise to avoid that person or organization. There is a fine line between observation and judgement, and letting any trust issue rear up. The tell-tale sign is how much e-motion is attached. If we feel e-motional about the situation then we are still stuck in ego, we still have issue with what is happening around us. And why is e-motion spelt as such? To suggest "e" stands for energy and therefore e-motion stands for energy in motion. We will eventually observe, if we have not already done so, that we cannot rise above anything about which we are e-motionally charged. We need to be comfortable telling the difference between e-motion and the inner feeling of Spirit. The inner feeling is always at ease, there is no anxiety, no attachment to outcome.

The best results are always when Spirits can interact. Forcing a position prevents this from happening. When the position is forced it tells the world we are focused on outcome, not on purpose. We create a mini-battleground for the control of the available energy and it negates growth.

Here is another differentiation to consider: force is not to be confused with perseverance. Perseverance, when well intended, creates great results. Force does not.

When things go wrong in unrelated bunches the following could be the explanation: When our mind wanders we attract more of what we are thinking about, and while we are resonating in this area we are vulnerable to pulling in anything else out there that is also resonating on a similar frequency. When our thoughts stray, we leak energy. We need to develop a sense of constant monitoring so that we do not leak energy for too long before taking back control.

Is this all starting to sound like too much work? There is a lot going on around us in the form of other peoples' energy bouncing around, and the general buzz of life. It is a challenge to keep our balance at all times. Our lives are not something over which to expect perfect control of, body, mind, and Spirit. However, the better our management, the more enjoyable our life experience.

Things to watch for

It is critical to understand energy as it relates to our existence. The failure to align energy in a positive sense that serves us and others well leads to stress. As our thoughts turn negative we just attract more of what we are focused on until we choose to change direction, and preferably, we make that choice before we experience unpleasant circumstances.

Everything needs energy in order to exist, so if we do not like what is happening we start by not feeding the experience energy. Remember the Cherokee Legend and the wolf you choose to be. As soon as the experience comes up we switch our thoughts to something else. Create a "switch to something else" prepared thought so that your reaction is swift when you catch yourself straying. I have an old tape by the late Jack Boland in which he talks of not liking his old schoolmate. He would see this schoolmate driving around town in a fancy new car and that was like rubbing salt in the wound. So Jack decided on a "switch" and every time he saw the schoolmate in the car he would immediately think of his grandson and smile. Eventually he was able to watch the car go by without angst, in fact he was happy for his schoolmate's good fortune.

Be aware of your reaction to people and events. Your reaction directs your energy and the rest of you must follow – body, mind, and Spirit. Do your best to feel your way through situations. The inner sense comes from Spirit doing its part to guide you. When you do react do not confuse feeling from within with emotional reactions, which are full of feeling sensation, but represent the ego and not Spirit. The urge to be angry, to judge, or criticize are immediate clues that ego is attempting to run the show. Remember, we are vulnerable to other peoples' opinions. When we feel challenged it is just that, we are being challenged about who we are, where we have placed our faith. Our reaction speaks to who we are.

What not to do with our energy

Always have thoughts for something, never against something. When we go against something someone is doing or planning, we are giving that something energy by focusing on it. Decide on an option that works for us and focus on that option, promote it, make it our intention then it will receive our energy and it will grow, instead of the idea that someone else is promoting.

A word of caution. When we act out of a sense of urgency there is fear involved, a fear of getting the outcome right, of not losing, or something similar. The results will reflect the belief behind the urgency. Act from the feeling sense of knowing what is good for you. I cannot emphasise this point enough – it is about feeling Spirit, not reacting with e-motion.

Flowing any negative thought risks revitalizing other negatives that are temporarily dormant, whether they have been that way for a day, a year, or more. This is on the principle of attraction, like attracts like, so think negative and more negativity will flow.

If we focus on the large grey cloud casting a shadow on our life we will lose sight of the fact there is sunshine on the other side waiting to break through – our "silver lining" – the gift that is ours if we are open to receive. Are you open to receive? Of course you are – or are you? Check the results in your life, and then check your wish list. The difference is the amount of interference you are running for yourself, getting the wrong information printed on those copies, putting out the wrong vibration, which is then returned to you. You are the originator of your own mail.

We often place a great deal of importance on something in our lives in the course of our preoccupation with our outer world. Our energy naturally flows that way because we are focusing in that direction. Some things, or people, take on a larger than life importance. We see them as more important than ourselves. This is very dangerous ground. We have given away far too much of our energy and sense of self and left ourselves vulnerable. When something goes wrong with that person or object it is like an earthquake – very damaging. We react to events surrounding the object of our attention and feel very threatened because something so important is not working well. What can disturb us, the loss of a cherished loved one without whom we do not think we can live, the loss of a job that we consider all-important (maybe the job consumes us and we have become a workaholic), or maybe we fear a crash in our financial investments. They are all about energy flowing out of control.

Does someone or something, such as government, push your buttons? Remember, that on which we focus grows, only in this case, if the situation or experience is not serving us well, the negative energy inside grows. When we focus on something or someone we risk drawing in the related energy. We would be wise to look at the situation so that it can be released, or we risk our health.

When we move forward in love and faith, doors open. When we move forward in fear our energy is wasted and we cannot reach the ultimate possibility. Energy is leaking out and we become drained. Over time that affects the physical health of our body. Health has so much to do with the way we flow our energy. Resistance in an electrical line causes burnout and the same thing happens to the body. Resistance and fear put a strain on our bodies. When symptoms appear we tend to focus on not being well, which brings on more poor health, and so we go down a slippery slope.

Choose to stay out of judgement for that is the quickest way to get drawn into energy outside of ourselves. Instead observe, observe, observe.

The energy you put out pulls in your experience of life

I find I receive easily most of the time, and if I do not get what I would like I know that I am not focusing my energy correctly. An old movie is running in the ego theatre and is getting in the way. How we flow our energy needs to be clear. Mixed signals bring mixed results. Do not broadcast in a storm so to speak, as in times when we are angry or frustrated. The extra e-motion attached magnifies the results, positive or negative, and when anger or frustration are involved it is most likely going to be negative.

To refute these concepts is to give our life over to ego and the pain we are carrying in our e-motional self-image. Life is as easy as we choose to make it. You are the creator of your experience, events are not just "happening" to you. The energy you put out pulls in your experience of life. Some people are already living life on their terms; some will seize on this information, act on it, and move on quickly.

However, it is my observation that most of us are plodders, whether we want to admit the fact or not. Whether we have been pursuing a spiritual path for years or not, most of us plod on. We all achieve change, but I personally have known only one person who has consistently challenged what is happening in her life and done something about it. Just one. The key word here is "consistently."

We need to remember that everyone is on his or her own journey. Meddling in the energy of others interferes with our own energy. Remember too, what we do unto others we do unto ourselves, for we are One. Interference has consequences; interference can change the energy flow and disrupt the spiritual intention of another.

We can see from the above that not all that we learn is detrimental to how we express ourselves in our adult world. We can have many positive examples. However, if our basket of experiences is weighted too heavily to the "negative," then life will have more than its share of challenges. However, these challenges are opportunities to encourage us to look at ourselves and heal that which has happened, through compassion, forgiveness and love.

How we flow our energy is intertwined with our ego and we need to understand how they work together.

Chapter 7

The Big Cover-up
(What we do to hide from ourselves.)

"Habit is a hell to which we cling in an attempt to stop the flow of change".

– Carolyn Myss, Anatomy of the Spirit

What we do to hide from ourselves

What is meant by the title The Big Cover-up? It is the lifestyle most of us choose, consciously or subconsciously, so that we do not have to confront the possibility of who we really are. Ego is in charge, for the most part. It is keeping us busy through Do-ing instead of Be-ing in touch with Spirit.

We get onto the treadmill of life and leave precious little time for nurturing our Spirit. It is easy to do; young families in particular have their hands full, and the single parent faces an even greater challenge.

We tell ourselves we "have to" do this or that. We become absorbed in other peoples' priorities, and hence their energy. This increases the sense of pressure as we spend more time away from our connection to Spirit.

When our equilibrium is challenged we often react in self-defence. One of the common things we use is anger. We use anger to cover up our pain when we do not get the outcome that matches our belief. We keep the focus out there and off our pain so that we do not have to consider healing the pain inside. Anger is about not being heard, and we simply do not want to hear our own cry for help. Anger immobilizes and keeps us off balance.

Angry outbursts add guilt to how we feel at a sub-conscious level. We know inside that blowing up is not doing us any good and is painful for the person on the receiving end. Yet, a large part of society seems to accept anger as something everyone holds and that it's an okay part of our being. Angry outbursts are not okay in most situations. Unmanaged anger is one of the most damaging aspects of our humanness. Anger is a big red flag being waved saying, "I need help, I am in pain."

Anger comes in many forms. In our observations of ourselves we must be aware of criticism and irritation, which can be less obvious forms of anger.

Some people are so angry they are afraid of the world finding out, so they suppress it. They are charming, and all the while that anger is eating them up inside and invariably shows up as dis-ease within their bodies, or as depression.

Anger creates a ton of static in our energy field, making it very difficult for Spirit to get through and guide us. We need to get a hold on our anger to enable ourselves to allow healing possibilities to come into our lives.

Nobody can make us angry without our permission

Another misconception that is widely held is that anger is an emotion over which we lack control. Those who hold this belief the most are often people who have the most anger. Alternatively, the victim attitude is that he or she "made me angry." That is not the case as anger is a chosen response. It is the dis-ease of "I do not want to change, I do not want to look at my pain." Anger is a major emotion and reaction.

We unconsciously choose anger as a reaction to our circumstances. Our own energy is drawing in experiences to bring to our attention that which we need to heal; this point is repeated with good reason. It is a key to our healing journey. We need to recognize what is going on as we observe ourselves.

It is hard to stay tuned in to Spirit if anger is interrupting our lives. Anger rears up in our life to protest and protect. Taking control of our anger and healing what lies behind the anger needs to be a priority.

Moving anger to the sidelines is a major necessity in order to clear the static for our healing journey. (Readers are advised that there are many readily available books and courses on anger management.)

Health issues and addictions

We choose many other ways to keep busy and avoid the possibility of change, which could lead us to truly getting to know ourselves. We cling to the security of what we know – better the devil we know than the one we don't. We put up all sorts of resistance to change, and at times excuses flow in abundance.

Our focus on our poor health issues gives us a prime opportunity to divert attention. Our focus also sends energy to our health issues and helps keep them around. When we are hobbling around with a cast on it is hard to ignore, but is the focus on where we are, or on how to get past the situation? Do we make the best of the situation without complaint and see ourselves healed soon?

Then there are the disturbances of the mind. If we sink into a low-grade depression then the focus is often hard to change. We feel down and have little energy to focus on getting back on track. It is a vicious circle, and one we need to seek help with before it becomes too entrenched.

Our various addictions keep our time occupied, whether they involve substance abuse, work, food, etc. All prevent us from spending time with the most important person in our world – ourselves.

Poor choices about what we put into our bodies – whether drugs, alcohol, or junk food, – lowers our vibration and our ability to, once again, connect to our Spirit within.

The blueprint we are living is very controlling if we allow it to be. That ego drive is like a repetitive drama, and some people add a lot of external spice to that drama. Some of the celebrities we know of do things to garner more than a reasonable amount of attention. More than one celebrity has admitted to attracting the wrong sort of man, a man that is abusive. They exit a relationship with one and promptly attract another, despite recognizing their pre-disposition. Drama does not just happen to film stars. Drama is happening with our friends and neighbours. Just observe, it is all around us. Some of us keep lots of drama going in our lives to avoid the pain. Rather than working to change ourselves, we create all sorts of change in our lives to occupy our minds and emotions – new jobs, moving to a new home, changing partners, or over committing our time. This all contributes to keeping us separate and obscuring our true identity.

Some of us are not given the privilege of having much discretionary time. Too many people are in survival mode, working two or three part-time jobs to make ends meet. It is a sad commentary that anyone should be struggling in the western world. It is hard to relax and trust in Spirit in such a desperate environment. Such situations do not leave us feeling that we have much choice.

Some people are not content with what they have and put themselves on a treadmill to have more, and the best example would be possessions. It goes back to the core belief that there is "not enough." This belief becomes a habit to which we cling, despite improvements in our circumstances. Some people have improving circumstances but then go out and buy a bigger house or an expensive car thereby raising, in their mind, their survival threshold. They do this rather than experiencing prosperity in more modest surroundings, because they need to maintain the sense of struggle that goes with believing there is not enough.

We are constantly attracting the challenge to change and choosing instead to look elsewhere. Some strive to be perfectionists – what a great sinkhole for energy! Never satisfied, they are in effect criticizing themselves. A great deal of time can be lost on this aspect of Do-ing.

Trust and abandonment

Trust and abandonment issues come from having been hurt in past relationships. How are these issues showing up? Do we stay out of relationships to avoid a repeat exposure? We avoid many aspects of our lives so that we are not exposed to pain. Avoidance, avoidance, avoidance! We then speak out with all the reasons in the world to support the position we have taken.

We suffer when someone important in our life places his or her judgement on us and we accept that judgement. We continue living with that belief about ourselves. We support that judgement with energy resulting in more energy and time lost.

Attachment to results

We sometimes get focused on outcomes in life and when we become attached to outcomes we create fear for ourselves. By all means have intentions, but not rigid goals. In order to bring about our rigidly held vision we will be tempted to manipulate situations and ourselves. These aspects of our humanity all contribute to keeping the ego-driven mind active and our Spirit suppressed.

We want to feel assured about the outcome before going into action, but this is akin to having a crystal ball for our life. This is not choosing life, but rather, choosing to live in a world of fear. Life offers no guarantees, but we seek them nevertheless.

Anywhere but in the present moment

We spend time gossiping or criticizing others – more time down the drain and an avoidance technique in operation.

We avoid challenges for fear of failure, of exposing a perceived inadequacy we feel inside. Holding back in fear is another avoidance technique in operation.

We are so often invested in avoidance of change, and yet change is always with us, always all around us. Do you play it safe? Do you avoid rocking the boat? All such activity is geared to avoid being confronted with the challenge of change. We may be afraid of a change in our practical circumstances or of a change in our emotional outlook.

Some people spend a lot of time attempting to please others instead of pleasing themselves. Only you can truly take care of you. Someone else might provide care for your physical being, in part, but only you can take care of your Spirit.

We seek comfort zones in our lives in order to avoid change. Ego will direct what those comfort zones will look like so that it is not challenged. We busy ourselves with changing the world outside of ourselves in order to satisfy our inner perceptions of what we need.

When we wander into a state of wanting we are denying who we truly are, we are declaring a state of lack, and letting our energy look to the future, where it cannot serve us. More time lost by not being in the present.

And so our life goes on, we spend much of our time being anywhere but the present, led into a world of avoidance, time wasting, and resistance by our ego, which wants to avoid any connection to the present. Our minds are kept busy, where ego plays. This diversionary activity puts a smothering blanket over the real person inside.

Chapter 8

How We Show Up In Life

Not to be able to stop thinking is a dreadful affliction.

– Eckhart Tolle, The Power of Now

Life is like a river, flowing ever onward to the ocean. Each of us is like a small stream that joins with another and another, all contributing to the abundance of the ocean. All that we are goes into the stream – our hopes, joys, passions, heartaches and tears, and more. There are many little streams, but as they come together they make for large rivers and eventually an ocean. Every contribution helps make the whole – the ocean. Every contribution is important, for without billions of small contributions there would be no flow.

With billions of people around us it is easy to feel lost. There is so much energy bouncing around in which to find our balance; so many people and corporations seeking a piece of us. Life is really about our relationship with ourselves. It is the only world we can hope to successfully control. How well do you show up for yourself? How well do you nurture your Spirit, care for your body, and pursue your dreams, ambitions, and intentions? Do you put yourself first in your life? I sense that our younger generation are doing a better job of this than the older generations. There used to be this attitude that to put yourself first was selfish. Well, no one else can be first for you. Life is about relating to you in the best way possible. When you nurture yourself well you then become stronger and have more to give. You will run out of energy if you are giving without taking good care of yourself.

A brief compilation of our attributes and challenges

Below are two paragraphs listing some of the things that we can experience in our humanity. One asks us to reflect on the positive things already happening in our lives. The other is there to help prompt some thoughts as to what needs to be healed. There are no right or wrong experiences. Remember, we are, thankfully, all unique in our expression into life. I suggest spending some time reflecting on the possibilities that emanate from the second list. This is just a stepping stone in the healing process. (Remember to avoid becoming stuck in "analysis paralysis.") The information you develop now will be relevant later.

Give yourself a bunch of ticks for all the beneficial attitudes and conditions in your life, such as:

Soothe Your Soul

- abundance
- affection
- alert
- ambition
- approval
- articulate
- attentive
- awareness about self and others
- benevolence
- caring feelings
- celebration
- comfortable touching
- common sense
- compassion
- competitive
- composure
- confidence
- conserving – not wasteful
- consistency
- creative
- decisive
- diplomacy
- discipline
- empathy
- encouragement
- energetic
- enjoyment of family
- enjoyment of friends
- enthusiasm
- family-orientated
- fellowship
- flexible
- fun
- generous
- gentle
- genuine
- goal-orientated
- good communication skills
- good listener
- gratitude
- happiness
- hobbies
- honour
- humanitarian
- imaginative
- independent
- individuality
- inspired
- intelligence
- introspective
- intuitive
- involvement
- joyful
- kind
- laughter
- love of family
- love of nature
- love of self
- love of surroundings
- loyalty
- modesty
- observant
- optimistic
- passionate
- patient
- peace of mind
- perceptive
- perseverance
- practical provider
- reasoned
- relaxed
- reliable
- resilience
- responsibility
- romantic
- self-reliant
- self-control
- self-esteem
- sense of self-serenity
- social life
- soft-spoken
- spiritual discovery
- spontaneous
- stability
- tactful
- talents
- tender
- thoughtful
- tolerance tranquility
- volunteerism
- wisdom

As well, recognize your ability to:
- bounce back
- express desire
- follow through
- give
- let go
- plan your daily life
- receive love
- relate to others
- socialize easily

Now consider whether any one, or more, of the aspects or conditions of human behaviour below have affected you in the past and whether they are still present in your current life. If they have truly been left behind, wonderful; if not, take a look at how they are influencing your life today.

- abandonment
- abuse
- addictive behaviour
- afraid of being left out or ignored
- anxiety
- anger
- apathy
- arrogance (the question is would an arrogant person recognize themselves?)
- burdened
- chaotic
- cold
- compulsive
- conceited
- controlled / controlling

- drug use
- egotism
- envious
- exaggerating
- fear of death
- fear of living fully
- fear of losing
- fear of losing a partner
- feel like a failure
- feeling inferior to others
- flirtatious
- frigidity
- frustration
- greed
- guilt
- humiliation

- laziness
- lethargy
- like to always be right
- loneliness
- loner type
- martyrdome
- obsessive opinionated
- overbearing
- perfectionism
- phobic
- poverty
- pretentious
- promiscuous
- rebellious
- reclusive
- regretful
- rejection

- critical
- cruel
- cunning
- cynical
- deceitful
- demanding
- deceitful
- depression
- disciplinarian
- disobedient
- disrespectful
- domineering
- doubting your ability
- dreaminess
- drinking regularly
- humiliating others
- hypocritical
- idealism in relationships
- impatience
- impracticality
- incest – perpetrator or victim
- indecisive
- independence
- inflexibility
- insulting
- intolerance
- irritability
- jealousy
- judgement
- resistance
- rigidity
- sadistic
- sarcastic
- secretive
- smoker
- smug
- stubborn
- submissive
- trust issues
- vanity
- vengeful
- vulgarity
- withdrawal
- workaholic
- worry

Let us look at the first item on second the list – abandonment – an issue for many people. There are three initial aspects to abandonment. The first is historical: were you ever abandoned? This could involve a physical abandonment by a parent through a physical absence for any reason, following a divorce or death, for instance. The impressionable child who does not yet have the ability to reason often will view the death of a parent as abandonment. There is also emotional abandonment. A parent can be physically present and not fulfill a child's emotional needs. They can be there, but uninvolved.

Second, do we act out on this? What is your reaction when situations or relationships do not go as you would like? Do you turn your back on them and abandon the situation?

Third, are we experiencing situations where other people seem prone to pull out on us? The energy revolving around this issue is causing it to surface in our lives, either through the way we express into life, or how others express to us – or both.

And if we have an abandonment issue, we might well be acknowledging, further down the list, that we have a trust issue. A trust issue will also often be present when there is an abuse issue. Abuse is the next item on the list. If our early experience in life included abuse, then abusive behaviour, either outgoing or incoming is likely a part of our lives.

If you "feel" such abuse is part of your life I suggest you acknowledge it now. It might not be present in your daily life; the abuse might be so painful that you have repressed it. Do your best to be honest with yourself. Do your review in a calm place so you can feel for your responses. It is not something to be done with the TV on, or the radio, or with other people present. Choose an opportunity when you can have peace and quiet. Turn off your computer and the ringer on the telephone. Give to yourself a total commitment to peace and quiet.

You may wish to only respond to those items that get your immediate attention. This is not a test. It is just something to help you identify what needs healing. You are the most important person in your life, so be prepared to help yourself to the abundance of life.

If you bring up more than you feel you can handle, then a visit to a professional could be helpful.

Chapter 9

The Mirror of Life
(The source of identifying the things to change.)

"There is nothing scary about life if you are not attached to results".

– Neale Donald Walsch, Conversations with God Book One

Life around us is a perfect reflection of who we are in this moment. As we look out at the reflection in the mirror that is the world around us we see ourselves, whether we care to believe it or not.

So what does this mean? First we need to remind ourselves once again that we are Spirit having a human experience, and it is that human experience that is so apparent in our minds and in our lives. Our Spirit is connected to Oneness, but we are each having our own unique experience of life on this planet. We interact with each other in order to have that experience. The life we lead in our body is ours, and ours alone, to experience. You and I are totally responsible for the results we achieve. Nobody can lead our life for us. Other people have influenced our lives and from that we have adopted a point of view or a belief. It might not have been a conscious choice, as it would be the case of a child who does not have the power of reason.

Are we serving Spirit, or serving an illusion?

Here we are today, enjoying life, or struggling with it, or more likely a bit of both? How do we improve our lot? If things are serious we go for professional help. If we are in a normal state of being we can use our own powers of observation and see if we can improve our life through some healing and letting go, thereby creating more space for connection with Spirit. As our outlook goes, so goes our life. Remember, energy flows to where the concentration goes. Our Source has given us incredible power, which we can tap into to change our lives. We have become so wrapped up in the world around us that we have lost sight of whom we are. We have gathered things around us that are important to us, but they do not necessarily reflect our Spirit's desire. Many things are created as an expression of our ego's desire. We are serving an illusion when we lose sight of who we are and give our energy away in a way that does not serve Spirit. You are the only person that can be in charge of your life and a catalyst for change.

How do we know what to change?

This chapter seeks to provide an answer for that question. Our energy draws to us people or events that reflect what is going on inside. Our mind can deny this all it wants, however, this takes us back to tuning in the radio – whatever station it is set to will bring in the reception we choose. The radio station has sent out a signal and like-minded listeners pick it up. We are the transmitter; we are our own little radio station and we are being tuned into by like-minded people and situations.

Be aware of what our radar picks up around us, for in the mirror of life we are always looking at ourselves. Our reaction is our expression of who we choose to be. All too often our reaction is judgement. We point a finger at someone in judgement. Now hold up your hand and point a finger at something with a judgemental attitude. Do you notice you have one finger pointed out and three curled around pointing at you! It is time to pay attention to what is going on around you, for whatever catches your attention is usually about you. There is so much to learn about ourselves in the mirror that is life.

Life is a perfect reflection of what is happening inside

The mirror of life around us is a perfect reflection of what is going on inside. If this is hard to believe then we are in resistance, and that is okay. That is the first thing that comes up when ego does not want to change. Writing this book has at times been a challenge. I am going over subjects that I understand to be true but which my ego vehemently resists. I have felt tremendous resistance at times because I am touching on subjects that my ego chooses to control. I am talking about the death of the ego, but then the ego is just an illusion I have bought into. You and I are in the same big boat; we are just sitting in different seats. We are rowing in the same expanse of water. We are in this together, for we are One, but individually our experiences are unique.

Life is a mirror that we have created in order to have the healing opportunities that we need in order to make different choices about who we are Be-ing. This mirroring gives us clues as to what needs to be healed in order to discard old beliefs that are not serving us well so that Spirit can have a greater influence in our lives.

Our circumstances may appear chaotic, but, in fact, our situation on this planet has been organized in a very precise way by a higher power. That way is based entirely on energy flows. We are energy. When we look out at the mirror of life that surrounds us we are looking at ourselves. Whatever we spot, we have got. Whatever we are projecting goes out, around, and comes back to us. Anything that disturbs or irritates us, which is basically anything that we notice reflecting back to us in our world that irks us, is something that we own somewhere inside, whether we like the idea or not.

Once again, we may not act out the same way, but sometime, somewhere in our life, this experience has been visited upon us and the experience has become a part of our emotional makeup. The experience has been carried forward in our sub-conscious bank of experiences as an unresolved issue. It still puts out energy, so we attract like circumstances to remind us of the healing that is needed.

My objective is to demonstrate that concept. The experience could be pleasant, so we may not want to change it. On the other hand, if someone is acting in a way that offends us it is time to pay attention. Ego would have us turn the other way. I say it is time to take charge of our mind and start a new thought process. This does not mean that we continue to act out in the same way. This is a key element to understanding this philosophy.

Here is an example: Jennifer is upset with Harry because she thinks Harry acts in an irresponsible manner. Jennifer does her best to act responsibly in life, so she distances herself from Harry because she does not want to be associated with such behaviour. What Jennifer is missing is the fact she has an unresolved issue with responsibility. She leads the life of a solid, responsible citizen. Inside, her emotional make up is calling for a healing. Jennifer's father deserted her and her mother as a child and whilst she has mentally put the desertion behind her, she has not emotionally forgiven her absentee father for his lack of responsibility. This is complicated by the fact she has reunited with her father and he is now very much a part of her life and now acts in a responsible manner. So Jennifer does not consider going there; in fact she is unaware of the issue. Why would she dig into the past when the present is working? We do so because the event from the past still hurts deep inside and every emotion we hold in takes energy that could be sent elsewhere to serve a better purpose.

Our feelings can rest dormant for years. Sometimes we are not even aware that they exist. I got a surprise one day while attending a seminar on financial prosperity, except that the messages from the podium went well below the surface and beyond the financial subject. One question was "Do you associate money with sadness?" It was like a bolt of lightning had hit me – the tears flowed, they poured. The situation that came up had never occurred to me, but I had been holding the sadness inside for years. There was another Brit next to me doing the same thing, and we Brits are not known for showing our feelings.

Our resistance to anything takes energy. Spirit is about allowing the river of life to flow. There is interference in the flow when we hold onto something like I was doing, or like Jennifer was doing. When we resist, when we hold on, we are dragging ourselves down. Jennifer is in a Catch-22. Life with her father today is good, but the inner child still hurts and needs healing, which causes her to react to situations where she observes a lack of responsibility.

Harry's lack of responsibility is not something that Jennifer emulates, but she still has the issue, and it relates to her father. That is why the mirror of life may bring up things with which we do not immediately identify. This is what I mean by owning what gets our attention; it is still a part of us, somewhere inside and it needs some TLC. The issue is not necessarily something we are currently being. In this case, Jennifer is acting just the opposite in her daily life; she is very responsible. However, lack of responsibility really catches her eye. She is more than an observer, she is still emotionally involved. This approach is very precise; it takes patience, understanding, determination and perseverance.

Does this seem like a lot of work? Yes it can be. We cannot get something for nothing. On the other hand, there will be two or three percent of the readers of this book that will grasp the whole concept and their lives will change overnight. They will grasp the big picture, seize onto living in "now time." and create remarkable changes. They will approach life "in the moment" and easily let go of the past when it comes up. For most of us, I expect, the changes will be less dramatic, but they will be important changes nonetheless. Once we start proving that this process works, our courage will take us forward to challenge more. Life will appear less daunting and we will embrace our Spirit more often and life will take on a new, exciting meaning.

Now it is time to watch out for clues in the mirror of life. The part that needs healing first is that which is catching our attention or our resistance today. That determines the order of healing. This is a useful guiding principle as to what we need to look at next. This is not a witch-hunt into the past. Remember, there is only one moment in time, and that is "now." Whatever is up in your mind now is what matters. If what is on your mind is not serving you well, check into it.

Anything that makes us feel uncomfortable is a clue. When we are feeling low it is often resistance to looking at something. If we think something is missing in life, check inside first. There are no solutions outside of us, only support for what we choose for ourselves.

Pay attention especially to events or people that irritate or make us feel angry. Remember we own it, somewhere inside. In this moment of recognition understand that you share something in common with the other person – show some compassion. Contemplate how you would be acting if you had walked through life in their shoes. That is something you cannot really do, because the shoes belong only to them, but be prepared to show compassion, as it is a key component for healing. Remember we are, in essence, One with that other person. We are just each having a different experience of life.

Ultimately, you are not creating a new you. The idea is to get ego out of the way and allow Spirit in to show you your potential for expressing your life, for creating and expressing the best of yourself.

This perfect reflection that surrounds us does not waste a moment. Everything happens for a reason, every meeting, every conversation, and every event. We need to step back and become the great observer of our own life. Always bear in mind that what is coming back to us is a result of the energy that we are emitting. We are creating our own circumstances. Our reaction is important. The choice is to accept the status quo or change our attitude. The change in attitude will change our energy, and hence our circumstances. It is how we flow our energy that is creating our world. You are but one person in this great sea of humanity on Earth, and at times you may feel lost. However, what you choose counts. One person changing out of seven billion will not significantly change the world, but one billion people deciding on a change will change the energy on the planet. It takes a billion individual decisions to reach this goal. If one person bails, there will be one short of a billion.

Ghandi was a man of great courage. He had an incredible desire for change through only peaceful means. His unwavering courage caught the attention of the masses and millions revered him. With this support, which included senior politicians, he was able to bring about great change although some of the consequences did not fit his ideals. He could not have succeeded in his efforts without the support of millions who identified with his ideals. One man alone with ideas cannot change the world.

Everything is energy and the ego also flows its own energy. Some of this energy can be beneficial; however, the areas that do not appear to serve us are the ones we seek to heal. The ego puts out its own energy signals and brings to us the circumstances that we need in order to heal the painful aspects of our life. Whatever the ego has latched onto in order to give itself an identity is in the mirror. We have the power to choose what we would like to change. On the one hand, ego is challenging and sometimes destructive. On the other, ego is giving us every opportunity to change by presenting us with a constant flow of clues, just waiting for the vigilant observer.

Here we can go back to the example of Jennifer and Harry. Jennifer's sense of responsibility is offended when she observes irresponsibility. It is an obvious clue using the mirror of life, but otherwise not an easily identified issue in need of healing.

We are, in one way, a potential slave to our ego and yet the ego is working to unseat itself. Ego's energy keeps pressure on us to change. If we fail to take action the resistance will show up in reduced energy or poor health. If we block the natural flow of life, something has to give.

We have a tendency to repress those feelings that are painful. We do not want to revisit those experiences and stir up old emotions in order to heal. So we suppress them, which requires energy. Over time we use up far more energy in suppression than we would use going through a short period of healing, even if it is painful. Unfortunately, many do not realise that most of these hurts from the past dissipate very easily when brought into awareness. We bring a wiser mind to the present moment and see them differently. Bring in compassion, forgiveness, and love; see the bigger picture and we are free to enjoy the energy that was required to suppress the pain. Sometimes it is that simple as we are holding on in fear because at some time we found in the pain something to fear. Of course, there can be many more traumatic events with great emotional attachments that are tougher to heal.

Once a few small changes have been made confidence grows. Once we start to align with the bigger picture we will gain momentum. What is the bigger picture for us, and the bigger picture of how we fit on this planet? We need to free the pain of the past and the associated fear. We need to realise that the past is gone and it really does not have a hold over us, only the power we give it with our mind. Some will grasp the bigger picture and let go easily, but most of us will take smaller steps. Energy plays its role in all of this. We are energy and we are surrounded by energy in motion. We are pulled many different ways in the average day, and subjected to many different energy flows. Not only are we putting out but also we are receiving, and much of this is happening automatically. Much of the time we are caught up in Do-ing. Some of it is serving ego, wasting our time so that we do not entertain the possibilities of life.

Now is the time for you to take greater charge of your life. You are the captain of your small but mighty ship, is it time to set sail on a new course? It will take loving yourself. You will demonstrate this through discipline and perseverance. You will stumble. Just pick yourself up, take a fresh look, let go of the past and BE in the moment. BE present to the possibility of NOW, the only moment that IS, this is the only moment in which you can live. It is a time to let go of fear, of those parts of ego that are holding you back, time to observe and take charge of your life.

Identifying what is in the mirror of life

There are many issues to be identified in the mirror around us. Here are some of the more common and obvious ones:

Trust is a core issue. It goes to the very root of our being. If we trusted in and acted from our being as Spirit we could live with ease. We have become separated from Spirit and have discovered fear. If we are having trouble trusting in who we are then we are more likely to find trust issues in the mirror of life. Trust issues are then compounded by our human interaction. There is so much mistrust in society. We are exposed to trust issues early on and they become part of ego. Why is it we have so many politicians in place who go on to prove to us they are not to be trusted? It is our energy that puts them in a position of power. Society as a whole has a trust issue for one reason or another. As a society we are not well connected to Spirit so we are reluctant to turn over our lives to Spirit and trust in something we cannot see. In addition, we have lost trust through adverse experiences. When we have a trust issue, we often attract situations where trust is broken and then we feel betrayed, and from there we spiral down. I have listened to many individual stories and been in many healing circles and I realize that trust issues are widespread.

Anger: Life is about energy and no emotion distorts energy reception more than anger expressed. It is so destructive. Anger management is an early stepping stone to gaining balance in life. The heavy presence of anger blinds us to possibility. Anger screams out saying there is great pain inside to heal, but while we are busy being angry we don't have to deal with it.

Then there is anger suppressed in the form of resentment. When people are being irritable or critical these are tell-tale signs that let us know people are suppressing anger on the inside. If anger is a significant player in your life, get help. An angry person is going to have more difficulty finding the inner peace necessary for the process of personal growth to take place. Healing can be likened to peeling back the layers of an onion. In order to get to the core of your Be-ing there are many layers, and one of the first that needs to go is anger. At least we need to get enough control so that we can function with an open mind.

Fear is the rope of bondage and is the opposite of love. Fear must be moved out of the way to allow love to flow.

Once fear is displaced love can be embraced. Throughout this book I maintain life is an inside job. We have displaced the Spirit, whom we really are, a Spirit that represents love, joy, peace, and abundance. We do not trust that this is so and have replaced that trust with fear, which brings on more fear. Ego thrives on fear and will strive to keep us there. We are exposed to fear right from conception. Fear is rampant and as its energy spreads so does its influence. In its extreme, fear leads to wars, of which there are many going on in this world. Fear keeps us down, on the defensive, afraid to risk. We need to overcome our fear in order to let love in. The humanity within us seeks to stop the fear that impedes the flow of the river of love, the fear that is at the core of our separation from Spirit. If we are experiencing fear in life then it is time to bring it into awareness and heal the cause of that fear.

Judgement serves no positive purpose other than it is perceived as a positive to the perpetrator. People usually judge down, not up. Praise is also a form of judgement; it's just more appealing. People judge down presumably in an effort to elevate their own sense of being. Judgement is far too prevalent in our society. It is easy to get caught up in judgement in little ways. It is better to observe; however, there is a fine line between judgement and observing. This is a time to remind ourselves of the Oneness of us all. That is a brother or sister that we are judging. Remember, we are putting out energy with that judgement. It follows that if this is a familiar trait then we have been subjected to judgement somewhere on our journey through life. Judgement does not serve anyone and is painful for the person on the receiving end. If we are experiencing judgement in our lives it is time to heal the subject.

Worry has never solved one problem and is mentioned again because of its destructive nature. What does worry do? It takes us out of this moment, out of the precious gift of life. Worry disturbs our body's energy balance as worry is based in fear. Worry is at the core of many illnesses and dis-ease in the body. Worry is one of the ego's greatest allies. It keeps us out of the moment by creating all sorts of imaginary possibilities in our mind. There is nothing productive about worry, and yet some people wear it like a badge of honour because they worry about so many people. They think worrying shows they care, so worrying must be good. Worry is an illusion and a complete waste of the moment – it is a waste of life itself. When something is on your mind check to see what can be done right now to help the situation. If no action can be taken in this moment it is time to drop the thought – just drop it until there is an opportunity to go into action.

Guilt is akin to the other end of worry. Guilt is based on some error we have made in our past. We hang onto the guilt and beat ourselves up until we are black and blue. Guilt is based on events of the past. Forgive the mistake, and the best we can do, after a sincere apology, is not to repeat the mistake. It is time to give ourselves a break. We are human. Maybe it will help to look at it this way – most of our emotions and experiences are learned from other people at a young age when we didn't have the ability to decide for ourselves. So is it someone else's pain we are expressing? Go easy – do not make guilt a cross to bear. It is another energy drain that leaves our bodies vulnerable.

Abandonment has been mentioned before. It hurts, especially when we are young. Abandonment leads to anger and a sense of not being good enough, and there are many other emotional downsides to abandonment – a whole book in itself. It is a subject people do not want to approach because it has those unhappy memories. But abandonment does need to be viewed in the light of the present moment in order that it can be healed.

Abuse is a more obvious aspect calling for a healing. It is a tragedy that humans treat each other in abusive ways. The abuse can be physical or psychological, leaving emotional or mental scars. The world feels unsafe. Abuse brings up the possibility of other major issues such as trust and not feeling good enough, of not being loved or lovable. This is another area where professional help is sometimes a good idea.

Addictive behaviour is an ongoing train wreck. There are many forms of addiction, some less obvious than others. Such behaviour is about escaping from the pain we do not want to relive in order to heal. It is tragic for the person suffering and the other tragedy is that people living around an addict are also affected, and this often involves children. We have to stop the cycle and it begins with the sufferer. Once again, professional help is available for many addictions. Most serious addicts live in denial. Then there are the millions that "use" substances as comfort and keep their intake within socially accepted norms and therefore it is viewed as okay. Addiction helps keep us in a low-grade depression, living below our potential. A couple of glasses of wine are socially acceptable, but when considered a necessity every night they can be the sign of a problem. It can be a fine line between the enjoyment of alcohol and its abuse. There are all sorts of comfort food and high on the list is chocolate. What real harm can there be in something that tastes so good? It really depends on whether you are "using" chocolate or purely enjoying it. Processed sugar is a factor in the huge weight problems in North America and elsewhere. It is in comfort food and, like most things in excess it is not good for the body. Excessive sugar will eventually impair health.

The saddest part is that others tend to make way for the more disruptive addictions and co-dependency becomes an issue. Once again this is a subject with all sorts of information and support available. This is another path that needs to be walked in order to heal. No stone should be left unturned. Ask yourself, "Are these habits and excesses serving me well"?

It is all about you

What is happening around you is all about you, the person looking back at you from the mirror on the wall. We are socially external in our approach to life, acting as if life is mostly outside of ourselves. The answers also start out there as clues to help bring us back to the centre of our being. Whatever the mirror of life reveals tells us how we feel about ourselves, it tells what is really going on inside. It is never about the other person, the event, or the accomplishment; whatever is taking place is a perfect reflection of what is going on for us. We are like a self-contained unit in this mass of humanity that has become dependent on the outside world. We are still part of the outside world, but currently we are more prone to DO things in the outside world than to BE in it. We are not consistently expressing from Spirit; instead we "do" into the outside world in order to exist and receive.

What to look for

As mentioned above, the clues to what needs to be healed are all around us. I prefer to look at what is going on today. To go back into history and dig up the past invites too much analysis. Remember that analysis paralysis invites ego in and so, too, does spending time in the past. The present day approach focuses on what is up right now. Once we zero in on something to heal, it might well cause us to look back for the solution and healing. But keep the path specific and focused. Focusing on the moment limits the energy and time we are expending to a minimum. Focus helps keep ego on the sidelines.

So step back and be the observer. Make note of what you like and dislike about what is going on in your life. Once you spot something, be prepared to own it because somewhere, sometime, what we notice has been an issue for us and that issue is continuing to send out a signal, it is burning energy. If this were not the case then we would be able to observe the situation without emotion, without judgement, without a strong desire to fix what is happening or get away from the situation. This approach of observing and identification is as precise as mathematics. This chapter focuses on identification; the next chapters help with what to do with the newfound information we are developing.

Where to look? The first mirror to look at is the one at home on the wall. This whole process of life starts and finishes with you. You are the master and the healer; you are everything to yourself.

It is time to check our feelings and habits. Do any of the issues mentioned above apply? Do you regularly feel moments of regret or worry, or feel victimised? Are you often defensive, do you feel a lack of something in your life, do you procrastinate or get angry easily, do you need to control what is about to happen in your life or can you let it flow? Do you like to live without risk; are you still smarting from a broken relationship? Do you gossip or criticize? These are a few possibilities to get started. Go easy on yourself, for most of us have pain.

Do not overload on things to review. The suggestion is pick maybe two or three areas for review at a time, otherwise our energy will become spread too thin. There is no hurry. There are no deadlines.

One objective is making life into one conscious ongoing meditation. We observe what comes to us in life, make no judgement about it, and decide how we are going to react to the situation from the most loving depths of our Be-ing. We decide how we are going to be in relation to any given situation, not what we can just do in response.

We pay attention to unfinished business, to things that irk us, for from under these issues great things can be revealed. The alternative is to leave the vibration out there in the Universe to keep on repeating and draining our energy.

Relationships

Relationships are a key mirror for clues as to what is in need of healing. Golden rule – don't try and fix the other person. This is about making changes for our own benefit. Be prepared for changes and opposition as you change. Everyone around us picks up our changing energy, consciously or sub-consciously. People have a tendency to find security in no change. Our close relationships are working in our best interests, whether or not we like what is happening. They are showing us what is truly happening for us, so do not run away. Instead, choose to grow away from the situation. We have heard of the divorced person who goes on to attract a similar person in their next relationship. If they did not grow and change, their energy is similar, so expect them to attract a similar relationship. This is a precise and exacting system in which we live and there is order in this apparent chaos. Only through changing our energy can we change the future. What we sow today grows tomorrow. What we experience today is a result of what we sowed yesterday. If the result is distasteful, then it is the result of our own "stinkin' thinkin'" as Val Van DeWall used to say.

Go easy on those around you. They have their own difficult journey; do not try and figure them out. Their life is their journey. The best way to help others is through example and let them come to us.

We apply the same basic principles already described to close relationships. The extra challenge with close relationships is that they are people who are more involved in our lives. There is a reluctance to risk and bring about change because the relationship might change. Many of us want to know the outcome before we commit to change. However, as said earlier, we cannot control outcomes. This is all about trusting Spirit to bring us our highest good, even though it may not feel that way as we are going through an experience.

Sometimes the challenge is in a relationship we did not have, whether it is the parent who passed away young, an early divorce or separation whereby the relationship with the parent has a gap of years, or of an adoption where the child receives genes of an unknown parent. Every child is connected to its mother in the womb even if it is not exposed to the father. It is tough to go back and find the solution when there was no physical event or interaction. Healing then comes down to dealing with the issue within our own self, observing something we choose to change and focusing on seeking a new outcome.

Most of our learning is done in the very early years of our life at a time that does not remain conscious in our youthful energy. If you still have your parents, then talk to them about those early years. In our youth we do not always see this need and the opportunity to share their perspective ends when they pass on.

The key relationship is always about the one you are having with yourself. You can learn so much by observing yourself. Think back on your conversations, your actions. Do you have regret about your actions? If so, you are, in effect, criticizing yourself. You do not even have to wait for someone else to pick on you – you are doing it to yourself. Sometimes we do not have to look too far for clues that can lead to healing.

The primary objective is to seek to align more closely with Spirit, which will change our whole outlook on life. Change is not about "if I do this I will have a better…" (whatever). It is about shifting to a different view of life. It is about expressing Spirit into Be-ing in your everyday activity, rather than carrying on as a human Do-ing.

Relationships go beyond the tighter bonds of family. We know teachers, ministers, and friends influence us. Sometimes it is just a single, profound meeting or event. There is also our social environment. It is a challenge to grow up in poverty and emerge with a prosperity consciousness. Some will go on to focus on money and through determination become financially wealthy, but that is just about money. A healthy prosperity consciousness is something quite different. Money is not the measure of prosperity. Gandhi and Mother Teresa are great examples of that. They believed in the flow of life; they never saw the need to acquire anything for themselves. Their lives were always about giving, accepting each day, and reacting the best way they knew how.

Social environment can, therefore, leave its mark. Some of our views of life are created through repeated exposure to something instead of a specific event or a particular relationship that leaves its mark on us. This is just one avenue for creating the feeling of not being good enough, the source of so much pain in many lives. We can come out of a wealthy environment and still feel there is not enough. Busy parents do not necessarily have enough quality time for children, or our academic achievements are not good enough. There are different ways we can inherit the feeling of not feeling good enough or that there is not enough of something.

Another behaviour we indulge in is giving out what we feel is missing inside of ourselves in the hope that it will come back to us to nourish what we feel is missing. Giving in the hope of receiving is done at the sub-conscious level. Our only real hope is to go within and heal the hole in our heart. We project our inner thoughts and beliefs perfectly. We need to understand this and tune into the clues that we are feeding ourselves. Some people flow love as they know love in order to receive love. Love and he/she will love me back and fill that hole in my heart. That is not a truly loving relationship as it is held together by a need for love. Love flows freely without conditions. Despite the greater possibilities, some people can find a balance with this and live happily with their circumstances. There are no absolutes in our uniqueness as human beings. There is another way that gives a different meaning to flowing love, one that feels so good, requires no effort and only seeks to give, not receive. It is the identification with Spirit that we truly seek.

Health

There is a philosophy held by many that there is a direct relationship between our spiritual, emotional, and mental well-being, or lack thereof, and our physical health. When our energy is being diverted from the natural flow of life it has to be stored somewhere in our bodies as resistance to flow. When are going against the flow of life it is like damming a river. Eventually, the pressure becomes too great, just like having too much water behind the dam, and it will burst suddenly. In like manner, the pressure eventually manifests in our body and our physical health falters.

Many turn to the conventional medical system. It is what we grew up with and it is the one that governments and medical plans support. Drugs manage or suppress our symptoms, but do not necessarily provide a cure. Alternative medicine is another source of managing symptoms. However, for a more complete healing, we will need to heal the non-physical aspects to support good health – our Spiritual, emotional, and mental outlooks, or the physical symptoms will likely return in time. The best presentation of this material I know of is by Louise Hay in *You Can Heal Your Life*. She has sold over thirty million copies, so there are many out there that follow her philosophy.

It is time to become your own observer, look around at what you are doing and saying and notice what others are doing and saying that irritates you or gets your attention. Gather the clues to what you need to change and honour yourself by making some changes for yourself. You are the only one who can do it.

Chapter 10

Forgiveness

To look good, forgive everybody. It's the best beauty secret.

– Jacqueline Bisset

As long as you don't forgive, who and whatever it is will occupy rent-free space in your mind.

– Isabelle Holland

The lack of forgiveness for oneself not only occupies the mind but also keeps the vibration out there, and that vibration can come back in different forms and in different relationships.

We have to develop some ideas of what we would like to change. We go about making change with compassion, forgiveness, and love. We are seeking to lift our fearful thoughts about life. We do so by embracing the opposite of fear, and that, as said before, is love.

First, let's be clear what is meant here by forgiveness. It is about forgiving the error another person has made, or that we have made. We do not have to condone the action that led to the error. Forgiveness is about letting go of a past event. It is a cleansing; we are quietly washing our hands of the past. Next, we forget about what we have released. If it slips into our consciousness again then maybe we are not finished with the subject. There is more than one level or aspect of forgiveness and this is explained later.

There are two approaches to forgiveness. One is the approach to those aspects of our life that we can connect to an event, past or present. The other is what to do when we cannot link present day events and emotions to a specific area to forgive. An example here would be the child that is given up for adoption or who loses both parents early in life. The child has been exposed to people at an age when they cannot be consciously recalled, but their influence is important. We do not know what that influence is, so we have to simply look at it in the present moment and make adjustments.

Will all this lead to a state of nirvana in your lifetime? No. Life is a journey, not a destination. It is for us to enjoy the stops along the way. This is about making the journey more enjoyable.

Explaining the need for forgiveness

The need for forgiveness arises out of a judgement we have made about life from our experience of it. It matters not that we were, say, two years old at the time. With our limited resources we made a decision about what was going on for us. It is time to let the experience go and come into the present moment. It is a major challenge to stay out of judgement, even when we have understood the negative impact it is having. To allow life to flow without judgement is a wonderful space in which to be.

Forgiveness is "for giving" back to ourselves a part of our life that we have lost because of our misunderstanding of what has happened in the past. We have been placing energy into a memory and it has become part of our persona. We have been putting energy into our sense of separation and it is time to forgive the error, to reclaim that part of us that is outside of ourselves, to simply let it go and allow love to flow from our Spirit. We do not have to make any effort for love because it is always ready to flow. It is now time for giving Spirit the opportunity by removing the blockage, the resistance placed there by our belief in something else about life.

Forgiveness invites in the higher energy of love, which embraces everything, when it is allowed in, and heals. Why is love so powerful? Because it is pure and flows easily. Because there is no friction or resistance. Love is the very essence of life itself. Matters of the ego involving fear require energy to hold them in place, because they do not flow naturally with life. Forgiveness is a conduit for love and to empower love in our lives. Forgiveness means not carrying the baggage of an experience. It means never having to look back, thereby creating freedom to live now. When there is failure to forgive, the energy around that experience keeps vibrating and the unhealed experience will keep coming back in different forms and different relationships, seeking the desired act of forgiveness. Remember, every sixty seconds you spend upset is a minute of happiness you'll never get back.

Forgiving others, forgiving self

If it will help to forgive, consider this: In order to fully appreciate joy, we must experience sadness; to fully appreciate inner peace we need to experience outer turmoil. There is a gift in every seemingly negative experience. The strict, controlling parent may stifle our sense of expression, but cause us to be disciplined in practical matters so that we easily get on with things that need to be done. The person that has bruised our heart is challenging us to find love through forgiveness. When we can forgive and feel love for someone that has seriously aggrieved us, then the potential of life can be experienced. The release will be a transformation.

After forgiveness is felt for with those around you, you are left with the one who really counts – you. Look in the mirror and go through the process all over again, but now focus on your relationship with you. It all eventually comes down to your relationship with yourself. Your own lack of forgiveness in your life will continue to draw situations to you like a magnet so that you can have an opportunity to heal. You simply have to forgive yourself for the erroneous judgments you have made about yourself based on your experience of life. Forgive yourself for believing in your own imperfections; forgive yourself for believing in your own persona seen as separate from Spirit; forgive yourself for believing in the ego trip, or ego deceit. It is all history and you can begin again in this moment. Not only does this need to be a conscious choice, but you must feel it is good for you. Your experience has been an opportunity for you to heal and come to a greater understanding of who you are. You need to see yourself lovingly, for the beautiful human being that you are. You have to do the same for yourself as was suggested in the healing process involving others.

You will find a need to heal within yourself because from time to time you will assume the cloak of that which needs to be healed and visit the experience on others. When this is recognized there is a tendency to feel guilty for the error. It is simply time to forgive yourself. It is too easy to look back and be critical of self or of others. You then take yourself away from the present, and if you simply dwell on the past then you are feeding it energy, the very energy you could be using to live in this moment. You are keeping the memory alive with your energy.

This all entails rattling the cage of the ego persona. The ego may not be serving you well but it, too, is not to be judged.

At the core of forgiveness is trust. We have placed our trust in the outside world rather than within. Now we seek to trust within; instead of something we can touch, we elect to place our trust in something we cannot see, only experience. It is a great leap of faith. In this leap I acknowledge that I am love, I am good enough, and I am open and willing to receive. I am not the person I have come to know, but a Spirit much grander, and it is time to let that other person go, with love. For to believe otherwise is to say I know better than my Creator.

In this process the old energy is released from my life, but never extinguished. There is always the potential for flashbacks because the energy of the event never dies. Our potential is to lay the event dormant in our lives and be vigilantly watchful for its return.

Combining compassion, forgiveness, and love

I now introduce three elements in the healing process: compassion, forgiveness, and love. We need to go further than acknowledging these mentally; we need to feel them, to know that they are in place in our heart. A young lady shared with me how she had challenged her parents for what she perceived as their errors when raising her. There was no doubt they were not perfect and could have done better. She got them to apologise for their errors and seemed to let the subject go at that. She forgave mentally, but did she do the emotional work? If she did not then the whole subject is still with her.

A compassionate start is needed. It helps me to flow compassion to remind myself that everyone is perfect and whole in every way except for the hurts of life. It is time to soften up and get out of judgement. We cannot speak for how well we would do if you had walked in their shoes. Remember we are One. Give some thought to how we would like to be treated if the situation were reversed. Set aside judgement and be ready to love this person, see past their human imperfection, and see them for the Spirit that they are inside, just like you. This is a tall order for some situations. We must get past this point if we are to grant ourselves freedom. Once we are feeling the desire to heal we can move forward to forgiveness. When we come to review our own actions, the degree of compassion should be the same – no double standards. There are actions for which we need to forgive ourselves.

It is time for giving to ourselves, and we do this by just letting go. Release the past so that it is no longer holding us back, drawing on our energy. Generate a real desire inside to let go of the past. What has happened is history; only our energy can keep the memory alive. Simply see the need to let go, do it, and move to the now moment. Wonderful. Some need to feel the letting go, to feel the sense of love toward the person that shared their pain with us. What is in it for you? Freedom. How do you close the deal? With love.

How do you know when the subject is done? You will know. There will be a quiet sense of inner peace and love all around the subject. You will feel complete.

It remains for us to be on guard, lest we get drawn in again. We have freed ourselves, but if circumstances come up to remind us of the situation we could find ourselves right back in it temporarily. Once we recognize what has happened it should just slip back out of our life with ease. We need to achieve memories without the attachment of a painful emotion.

Affirmations and imaging

We learn by constant repetition or impact. We can use the same tool that took us down to bring us back. As we work through the forgiveness process, repetition works. Creating a positive affirmation for ourselves that we believe in and that we can say with conviction and feeling is often useful. The affirmation needs to be repeated often, with feeling. Just speaking the words out loud or to ourselves has little impact.

Sometimes imaging can also be useful. There is no one approach that works for everyone. We are all unique, and what works for one scenario might not work for another. Imaging can be a powerful tool; it is even used with young cancer patients. One aspect of this is to heal the inner child by going back and experiencing the past, but imagining a happy outcome, one that would have left the child with a warm feeling. Another option is to visualise a warm picture of the person in the present. Alternatively, you may wish to create a vision to move toward in the future. The vision may be about another person or how you will react in a given situation. This, to me, comes under the heading of a switch.

A switch operates when we identify a situation and seek to change it by immediately putting something else before our mind's eye, something we feel is positive for us.

Is it all starting to seem like a lot of work? We will simply get out of life in proportion to what we put into it.

The tougher situation, in my opinion, is when we cannot identify a source for our feelings and challenges, when we look at the mirror of life and wonder what has happened to bring us to this point. There is nothing that can be recalled in the conscious mind to bring into the healing circle. So what then? First, we must own up and accept what is being mirrored to us. We need an awareness of what is going on around us; that is the first step. The mirror of life has revealed something to us. Now it is time to accept that life is precise and that, somewhere inside, we own what we observe. Give some thought as to whether we have visited this on someone. This would create a need to forgive yourself. Create a switch in the form of a new vision of action for you, and then back it up with an affirmation, said with feeling.

Try a three part affirmation:

> I AM love
> I AM loving
> I AM loved

or

> I forgive myself
> I AM forgiving
> I AM forgiven

or

I care for myself
I care for others
I AM cared for

Pick any subject for your affirmation; first give it to yourself, then give it away, and then be open to receiving. It becomes a circle. (This three part approach might not fit for all subjects.)

As we say the words we have a positive image in our mind's eye. It will add impact to the affirmation. If you would like to add power, then do the affirmation in front of a mirror, with eye contact. Mirrors can be a huge test. I can remember being in an impromptu healing circle one night. We encouraged Martha to move over to the mirror and say, "I love myself," and "I am worthwhile." She put up huge resistance and she refused to look at herself. With encouragement from all of us she finally tried it. It was a big night for Martha. It was apparent she experienced a major shift, but only she can speak to how effective it was for her.

So that brings up another possibility: working with a good friend. Let them understand what you are attempting to heal, let them help keep you focused. Let them hear your story, let them feed back information. This is not for everyone it is just another option.

Personally, I do a lot of journaling when I feel there is an issue coming up for me. Sometimes it flows easily. Sometimes I ramble, sort of relax and suddenly find myself writing something meaningful. If I end up feeling stuck I put my problem out in the form of a question. I absolutely believe in "ask and ye shall receive." The key is in believing. Release the question and an answer will come soon. The answer may not show up in a manner we are expecting, so we need to be alert. It could be in the next book we open at a random page, in the words of a song on the radio, in a movie, or it may just flash through our mind. I say flash because to me, when it gets the chance to communicate, Spirit is instant. A complete thought is delivered with clarity and understanding before my mind has a chance to engage what is happening. And that thought is felt inside, not just between the ears. In effect, Spirit has bypassed the ego because we cannot afford to have the ego filter get in the way. That is the way I perceive it, but you could have a different experience. However, I believe you will know when you know. There will be a sense of peace around the subject, a feeling of love and that all is well. It will not be an ecstatic party feeling, although there will likely be a feeling of celebration in your heart.

We have looked at the power of the now moment – the "present" of life itself. Stay, as much as possible, in the now moment. Let go of "mind chatter," the busy-ness of the mind. Stay focused on what is happening in front of you and quickly come back to now if your mind wanders to another time, to something that cannot be addressed right now. When you are present you are open to all the gifts Spirit is wishing to share with you. We heal through feeling, not through thinking. Thinking is of the mind, the playground of the ego.

We are seeking to create memories that, when recalled, do not stir unpleasant emotions. We have let go of the emotional attachment to what happened, however painful it was. It is in the past, and, simply, the past does not exist except in our mind. In this way we have total control over the situation. The past cannot come back. It can only repeat as a memory in a similar manner to remind us that the past has not been released. The past is not happening now. All that is happening regarding the past is going on mentally or emotionally inside us. We have to be feeding the past for it to even exist in our mind or emotions. It is time to cut off the supply.

When we are carrying memories we do not like, then we are living in regret, and that does nothing for us. If anything, the memory is taking away from the present moment.

Always remember to include yourself in forgiveness – go easy on you! You are included in all healing and another sometimes forgotten relationship for healing is the one you have with your Creator. We get mad at him/her too, for example, when we lose a child. It is hard to understand such a seeming waste of a life and it is easy to get angry. The total understanding of life seems to have been placed beyond our grasp, which makes being here seem even tougher. We have to accept that there are things beyond our understanding that will remain that way for our time on this planet. Possibly the worst dis-ease we go through is self-condemnation for acts we perceive to be wrong that we have done to others.

How do I change future outcomes? I make sure I have let go of ties to previous experiences. I let go and get in a groove that hums along with Spirit. I get out of my own way. I see others as having a different experience, maybe a difficult time. I see another person as One and in a state of abundance. There is always enough.

Questions to ask:

What is uppermost in my mind?

What do I notice about what is going on?

Is it something I like or dislike?

Is it something I would like to change?

Can I own it? Can I accept that, somewhere inside of me, I have lived through a similar experience? Either someone did it to me or I have done it to someone else, or both.

Can I clearly identify the issue?

Am I willing to do something about it?

Can I bring compassion to this picture?

Can I bring forgiveness to this picture?

Can I release it with love?

I say "picture" because visualisation is so powerful. We have a picture of something and the idea is to change how we feel about it. One way to help is to relive the event in our mind and visualize a different outcome.

We must be willing to make a complete change. A conditional change is just that – it is not forgiveness. It is moving the judgement of a situation to another viewpoint.

Can we find the compassion necessary to prepare us to forgive this experience in our life? Having compassion softens us up for the forgiveness process. If another person is involved we need to be able to see that person in a different light. We cannot just say, "I forgive you" and continue to think of the person as a jerk. They may still be out there acting that way, but we need to see past their personality, for it just masks their pain. We are seeking to separate ourselves from their pain. It is theirs to deal with so leave them with it. Somewhere along the line their energy was visited on you, causing you to make a judgment about life that has not been serving you well. Every scenario invites you to look and discover the opportunity that is on the other side. There is a sports saying, the greater the pain the greater the gain. Under that rock of pain you feel is the greatest ray of sunshine and feeling of joy. In releasing the pain you will experience the greatest joy and sensation of love. It is like a reward for the suffering. It is always someone else's pain we are releasing, pain that we have chosen to accept for ourselves. Pain that sometimes is visited on us in the harshest of circumstances.

When I think of harsh circumstances I think of an amazing woman I saw on TV a few years ago. As I recall it she was driving along and the man in the next car shot at her. The bullet went across her face and took out both corneas rendering her blind. He took her from the car to a motel and raped her. Early next morning someone saw her on the motel balcony naked and calling for help. Her husband subsequently left her and finances became difficult. She went on to be a public speaker. She was asked how she felt toward her assailant. I cannot quote her exact words but basically she said she did not waste a moment thinking about him. He had already taken enough from her and she was not going to give him any more of her life in the form of a moment of her time. The moment we are living right now is the only moment there is; she decided to keep it for herself and not throw it away. I think many of our perceived problems shrink when held up to that story.

She does not appear to have spent time in the process under review, she appears to have gone directly to focusing on the moment and excluded him from it. That is a powerful decision from a woman who had suffered so much, and it became a very powerful approach to life for her. If you cannot emulate her and go directly to the now moment, then another healing process is necessary. I acknowledge that some people have some brutal experiences in their history. So brutal that professional help might be the best route with which to start. If someone has brutalized you, then you might anticipate that somewhere in his or her history they have been affected in a similar way, or somehow their mental outlook has become distorted.

The pain visited on us by another is pain from which we need to separate. In an attempt to distance ourselves from the pain we use many names for those who have acted badly toward us. That is only a mental separation and the focus remains on the person and the associated pain. We may create a physical separation. Another person may go and be, but cannot stay and be. However, if we have not forgiven them, then the pain they inflicted is still with us through the vibration of energy, even if they are physically out of our life.

So, once we have viewed the situation with compassion we can move to forgiveness. Again, this is about letting go, not about condoning. This is being done for our benefit; it is not about making them feel better. It is about giving ourselves freedom to breathe in more of life. As we forgive we open up the possibility for more love to flow in our lives.

We are seeking a sense of inner peace with the subject and the person. We need to be able to flow love in order to experience the inner peace. When we feel it we will know we have accomplished our goal. This could take a lot of time, patience, and perseverance on our part. The effort will be worth it. It will free us.

Now we have successfully forgiven someone for inflicting his or her pain on us. We have forgiven ourselves for making a judgement about the person. Now, maybe more than one person treated us this way. It should be much easier to go through the process again. But did you, in turn, treat someone this way? Have you forgiven yourself for what you did? If it was serious, amends need to be made, in person where possible. The energy is sometimes wrapped up in different packages. We need to unwrap them all, otherwise the energy is still active and will show up again. Our first attempt at healing using this approach may take some time, but it will become quicker and its benefits will energize us. Eventually, we will see life differently; we will intervene in the process of life before anything gets out of hand. We will observe life instead of judging it; we will allow people their space whilst maintaining our own boundaries. We need to remove the sense of separation whilst feeling independent in ourselves.

Applying the principles involved

In each application of this process there can be several layers. Let us say Peter severely criticizes Annette and gets angry with her. Her first healing is with Peter. She also needs to look at what she may have done in the exchange that she might want to forgive herself for. She may have fought back verbally; maybe she hit back physically. She certainly needs to forgive herself for letting herself be treated in this way. When this is healed Annette needs to look at what happened in her history that gave her the energy that attracted Peter's abusive behaviour. When did she learn to be treated that way? Who treated her that way – family members, friends, or authority figures? She then needs to go through the same process of forgiveness with each person that has treated her in this way. Once again, she needs to forgive herself for any part she played in the process, or at least for accepting such treatment. She needs to let go of the pain she felt in the past when she was on the receiving end. There needs to be a sense of completion with each step.

We need to look at the current situation that triggers our reaction, and then look back for the original source to also be healed. This may involve more than once source. A lengthy process, you say? Yes it can be, and the rewards are equal to the effort that you are prepared to bestow upon yourself.

What if there has not been a specific event that we can recall (we were too young), or what if we feel less than our best because of something we have come to believe over time, maybe years? It could be years of being told we are not good enough, or being in a home where there is little money, being surrounded by poverty where we feel there is not enough out there for us. We may have been constantly ignored, or as the eldest child, been stuck with responsibilities beyond our years. This would rob us of some part of our childhood. Picked on at school? It all leaves an impression about life and how we fit in. When the origin is so non-specific we must turn our focus on ourselves. The learning was done over a period of time; the judgement that we have made took repetition before it was accepted as part of our being. The same approach is used to heal by using repetition of affirmations and visualizations. We see ourselves with abundance, then verbalise it. We create pictures to put on the fridge to see every day. We constantly affirm our new direction with love and enthusiasm and our new intention will come to pass. We are generating a new energy for ourselves and as we send it out into the ether of the Universe, so it must be returned to us. We create our affirmations, always making them positive. (Remember that the sub-conscious does not recognize the negative. Always put affirmations in the present tense and in a way that declares them as happening. Anything put in the future tense has no power. There is only the now. Starting an affirmation with "I am" is very powerful.)

In summary:
- Use the mirror of life to identify what needs healing.
- Ensure that we are approaching the subject with compassion in our hearts.
- Forgive the person currently involved with the situation or the person in the past.
- Forgive ourselves for our part in the event or for accepting the treatment.
- Look back for the original source of the need for healing; forgive the person involved and forgive ourselves again, if necessary.
- Just let it all go and bring ourselves into the present, a peaceful space where love is present.
- The forgiveness process can be supported by our overall daily attitude and actions, reviewed in the next chapters.

Chapter 11

Healing Attitudes

If you do not go within then you go without.

– Neale Donald Walsch, Conversations with God, Book Three

In this chapter I am going to share some thoughts to contemplate and hopefully some will resonate and provide food for thought. Some just take a sentence or short paragraph to share, so I have highlighted a word or two so that the topic is easy to find again. Managing our attitude will help keep us centred, closer to Spirit, in the moment and hence out of ego. Our attitude can always be changed, and therein lays the key to a different outcome. Here are some attitudes on which to reflect.

Recognizing Spirit

We can support our quest for alignment with Spirit by being aware of our attitudes. We set intention with our attitude, a vision of how we would like to be present in the world. We cannot change some things around us, but we can change our attitude. The goal is the unwavering belief that we are Spirit, and feel our Spirit coming through in every now moment. It is better we choose to flow with our all-knowing Spirit rather than submit to ego.

Faith

A key aspect of living with a healthy attitude is to understand where our faith lies. To believe there is a powerful Spirit constantly at our side is a blessing. It is a challenge to believe in something that cannot be seen, something that cannot be paraded in front of others as "proof." It is a blessing to accept that Spirit is here for our ultimate benefit. It is for us to give Spirit full reign in our life, to harness the power with which we have been blessed. Not only to be in the moment, but also have faith in what living in the moment will bring. Remember we are not human beings attempting to have a temporary spiritual experience – we are Spiritual Beings having a temporary human experience. Trusting in Spirit is a great leap in faith. It is a very necessary aspect of Be-ing. We let go of our story, simply let it go and trust.

Trust and doubt

It is difficult to have meaningful long-term relationships without trust, or to have a fully functional life because we are always in doubt. When in doubt we cannot possibly embrace anything fully and give it our full energy potential. We are constantly stuck in two minds, conscious or subconscious, and mixed feelings create mixed energy, which create mixed results. This leaves us frustrated and feeling out of control because the results do not always appear to serve us well. Actually they do serve us because they are pointing out the error of how we are focusing our energy. Putting our trust in Spirit can help us overcome this dilemma.

Feeling

Feeling is the expression of Spirit. We find answers when we go within and feel for answers. We will not find answers dwelling in the mind, where ego loves to operate. The essence of Spirit is feeling, not thinking. Thinking is for necessary practical matters. We need to do some practical thinking in our lives. This will, by necessity, involve reflecting on the past and planning for future actions. There is a constant risk of getting emotionally involved with what has happened in the past and fearing the outcome of future events. At times when we are emotionally involved with external matters we pull ourselves away from that centred part of us that is love.

Security

There is a sense of security that only comes through believing in Spirit. Once we have this belief then we will be able to tolerate insecurity. Once again, the insecurity is perceived and is outside of us. Live with knowledge there is a powerful Spirit at our side ready to help, just let her in, she is our security.

More than I know

I have learned there is more going on than I can hope to understand. I know that our Spirits are working behind the scenes to bring us enlightenment. Keep this thought in mind for comfort.

High self-regard

Be good to yourself. One of the best things we can do is refrain from criticizing self. Give to yourself that which you feel is missing, and give with feeling. Be prepared to give to yourself at least as much compassion and understanding as you would give to anyone else.

If asked the question "Who is the most important person in your life?" would you answer "Me?" Or would name say your spouse or your children or some other person? Only you can show up as number one in your life. Someone may make you number one in their life, and that is their error in consciousness. You are the most important person in your life so please treat yourself accordingly.

Loyalty – honour ourselves

Part of treating ourselves as number one in our lives is to be loyal to ourselves, to be true to those values we hold dear to our heart.

When we choose to demonstrate loyalty to someone else or a cause, because it is something in which we believe, we are honouring ourselves through our decision. If we overdo that loyalty we could end up subjugating ourselves to another person, and that is unhealthy.

The challenge comes when our viewpoint changes and we have to make changes around us in order to honour ourselves. This can create an upheaval around us because our present circumstances are based on being loyal to the views we had in the past, which no longer coincide with our new outlook. If change involves family or close friends it can be a rocky ride. If we fail to go for change we are stuck betraying ourselves. It could easily make us feel as though we are between a rock and a hard place. Always honour yourself for no one else can do it for you.

Avoid victim thinking

A person cannot feel like a victim unless they give themselves permission to feel that way. Easy to say, but it is tough to see a way out if you are the one feeling victimised. A person in the victim role abdicates some of the responsibility for life and tries to blame another or others for the events that are occurring. There is a need to recognize the consequences of the energy that has been put out in the past that is returning to us. Such a negative attitude creates more of the same.

Choice

Life is a series of choices. A key choice, underlying all situations, is between love and fear – the love flowing from Spirit or the fear emanating from ego-based beliefs. The one we salute in any given situation is important, for our choice will determine the quality of the outcome. If there is a sense of fear surrounding a situation or the outcome is uncertain, then this presents an opportunity to clear something from the past.

Openness to receive

We need to feel good enough about ourselves to be open to receive. Giving into life unconditionally tells us that we have enough to give. The Universe will seek to replenish and multiply what we have released. We give freely and at the same time leave the incoming door open. We cannot have issues on this side of the ledger. To hold back (with regard to anything) is to speak to lack, and that affects receiving.

Do not expect the cart to come before the horse with a load of goodies to make us feel better. We have to feel better about ourselves first, then expect the horse and cart to arrive with help. Our good does not come from outside of our being. A solution created "at home," within, is a better solution.

Happiness

It is not possible to go out and find happiness because it already exists within, but we can let go of the unhappiness we are harbouring. It is holding onto unhappiness that blocks happiness flowing from within. Happiness is our own responsibility and we only need to consider a change when we are not happy with how we are feeling.

Another expression of happiness is joy. Joy is an expression of Spirit. It too can only come from within. We choose to be happy or sad. A minute spent being unhappy can never be recovered.

Freedom

Nothing can jeopardise who I truly am without my permission. I live in freedom until I choose to surrender it and subjugate myself to the energy, opinion, or actions of another. The choice, as always, is mine, at least in our freer western society.

I can be incarcerated. However, it is only my body that is held. My Spirit is always free and I always have the freedom of choice. That freedom of choice is about my attitude in any given situation. Seek and you shall find; break things down and you will see that you are always free. Only you can bind yourself. Viktor Frankel, while held in various concentration camps during WW2, found comfort in seeking the meaning of life under atrocious conditions. His positive attitude was inspirational to his fellow inmates.

In similar manner, Nelson Mandela came out of twenty-seven years of incarceration without bitterness and demonstrating an unwavering attitude of peace. He went on to seek only peaceful solutions to South Africa's social and political issues.

Perfection within

To be concerned about being perfect "out there" is another drain on our energy. Instead, we can radiate perfection from inside and be with the feeling emanating from within, from Spirit. Our Creator sees us as perfection on a journey. Attempting to be perfect in the outer world puts us on an endless treadmill.

I often remember one of my favourite sayings, which is repeated in this book and on the cover because of its value, and which helps me calm down and bring compassion to a situation – everyone is perfect and whole in every way except for the hurts of life. Above all, I remember to give myself the same breaks I give everyone else – I go easy on myself.

Performance

It is a challenge, but I do my best to avoid measuring myself against the performance of others. We are all unique. Be satisfied with who you are. Comparing is another opportunity to fall into the judgement trap.

Health

Good health is a blessing and is to be cherished and never taken for granted. It is not wise to wait until our health takes a significant downturn to seek faith in order to heal. If we are blessed with good health it is a great time to explore who we are. It is sometimes difficult to recover from a serious health issue; therefore, preventative action is the wise thing to do. Paying attention to minor health issues provides clues to what is going on inside.

Acceptance

Be prepared to accept those things over which we have no control. Let them go, and replace them with the image of change that you would like to see. Manage your energy. I find it difficult to live in acceptance when I see so much need for healing in this world. I have to do what is within my capability and accept those things that I cannot change through my own actions.

Letting go

I have more power in letting go than I do holding on to any thought, for without e-motion the power of that thought will arrive via Spirit mail at its destination. With e-motion attached it will bounce back to me or get lost, because I have attached myself to the outcome. The most beneficial outcome will be distorted to the extent I have attached my own e-motional feelings, which are based in my distorted ego.

Willingness

This is a big door opener. Being willing leads to a lot of possibilities. Just be open to possibility, be willing to trust in the possibility. Be willing to change, to forgive, and to love.

Success

Define success for yourself so that you have a framework to refer to when you wish to assess how you are doing. This is an individual choice and remember, we cannot all be leaders. Our worlds, by necessity, are smaller. How successful are you in your world of influence? Most of us are in a routine, so we need to find our success values within that routine. How are you doing as a stay at home mom, an underrated occupation? Or do you have a rewarding vocation like nursing, or work to improve our environment? Is success being happy most of the time, or is it giving back to society in a volunteer capacity, or being a good grandparent, a good friend, a politician, a rich person, having a big house, or having a prestigious job? The list is long and we can choose what is important to us. A blueprint for our idea of personal success will cause us to look at the various aspects of our life and decide what is and what is not important in our success formula and start to make changes to align with that formula. Sometimes it will take time to get in line so be prepared to be patient. Getting to where you are took years.

Time

This is a tantalizing subject. We all have the same number of days in a year. Within the same timeframe, some people achieve far more than others. Time management is important and there is plenty of information available on this subject. However, our attitude toward time is also important. In our busy society it is easy to be left with the feeling that I do not have enough time. This feeling must give way to "I have plenty of time." We only have the now moment, the same as every other soul on earth. Thinking we do not have enough time creates a sense of lack, and guess what we create? We come to the end of the day with a low sense of achievement. Staying focused on what is in front of us is the best thing we can do to best use time. When our mind wanders off of the present subject, so does our life. A wandering mind is not present to the moment, so our life is lost temporarily – we stop living. We squander the very time that we desire.

The "Challenge."

A local dance teacher, David Joseph, refers to the next step to be learned as a "challenge," pronounced softly, as if spoken with a French accent – "shallange." It seems to remove the hardness from the word and makes the word challenge more welcoming. And that is what we need to do with our lives, make the next "challenge" welcome, and make it sound easier.

Change

And with every "challenge" comes the invitation to change. Change is at the very core of life, and yet it is resisted by so many. Change is an opportunity, not a threat. Change is to be welcomed. Staying within our present framework might feel like a rut, and a rut is just a coffin without a lid, which leaves us the opportunity to climb out. Change cannot happen if we choose to stay in our rut, doing things the way we have always done them. Repeating the same actions will always produce the same results. Remember too, it is not "them" that must change – it is you.

We need to be calm and centre our Be-ing during times of change. Be-ing is not a doing thing. Be-ing is the calm eye in the middle of the hurricane. It is the place of calm, joy, and peace. It is a place from which it is easy to go forward into the world with enthusiasm and express our joy in Be-ing.

Life is an inside job and calls on us to be centred. We spend much of our lives living in the outside world where change is constant. When the dust settles and there is calm, life is all about our relationship with ourselves. How are we reacting and expressing and creating into life around us? It all begins and ends with ourselves. Are we being kind to ourselves? How is our level of self-acceptance? If we get up and feel we have got out of bed on the wrong side do we criticize ourselves or do we look in the mirror and accept that is where we are at in this moment? It is time to let it be, to show compassion for ourselves, and allow ourselves to be human. To resist or focus on our negative feelings will give them energy and they will linger and take up more of our time. Just observe and move on with the day, for this too will pass.

What goes around comes around

This is a statement that is used often, and how true it is. It is an easy one to remember and we use it to remind ourselves that what we are experiencing today is the result of our thoughts and actions from our yesterdays. Through our thoughts and actions we are, in effect, demonstrating our desires to the Universe, and, like an obedient servant, the Universe responds in kind. It's a bit like what is sauce for the goose is sauce for the gander. If it was good enough for you to act on, so the Universe assumes that is what you like and serves you up more of the same.

Patience

There is so much more going on than you or I can ever comprehend. When we do not get the outcome we would like there is invariably a positive outcome that may not be apparent for a long time. Alternatively, the outcome may remain an apparent mystery because the benefit is something that does not materialise.

Results

When we want to know what is really happening in our life, check the results. Failing to reach a goal measures the degree to which we do not think we are worthy to receive. The quality of our results tells where we have an error in consciousness and need to do some homework and change our attitude.

When results do not appear to be going well they are not wrong results. We are still a bit stuck, and the disappointing results are actually clues to help us make the attitude adjustments so we can change our results.

A reason, a season, or a lifetime

Everything, yes everything, has a purpose. Be available to embrace the experience and be patient, for the reason for an experience can only be revealed when the experience is complete. Experience does her teaching backwards – she gives us the test before explaining the lesson. This might take a long time. Meanwhile, look for the gifts in the experience, the ones we can give to one another, and the ones we are to receive. Spirit comes to us in many ways. It has to have many avenues, because we block so many with our fear. The people that come into our lives and interact with us are a valuable part of our experience. They are there for a reason, a season or a lifetime.

In conclusion, we need to determine what we stand for, how we want to present ourselves to the world, what works for us so that we can experience love, joy, and peace. Then we need to adjust our attitude so that we rejoice in its feeling; we need to go forward and make something happen. We need to go into action!

Chapter 12

Action

My entire life journey ultimately consists of the step I am taking at this moment.

Eckhart Tolle, A New Earth

"What you have done is unimportant compared to what you are about to do."

Neale Donald Walsch, Conversations with God, Book Three.

Partnering with Spirit

We cannot get the education we desire without signing up and taking courses. If we choose to change jobs, getting out there and promoting ourselves adds energy and momentum to our decision. Actually, a job could come to us with just a change in attitude and I have seen this happen in an amazing way to a lady with whom I worked. However, in most instances, it will likely happen more quickly if we get out there with some enthusiastic energy to emphasize the new direction we wish to travel. Colonel Sanders, the founder of KFC, reached retirement age before he started the restaurant chain that has become so famous. It did not just happen. He worked tirelessly to promote his chicken recipe. He started a chain that is now the second largest in the world. He did not start with this as a vision; he started with the first step: selling his recipe.

It's time to send a message to the Universe to dictate the direction in which we would like our life to proceed. There is nothing like action to register a new direction for our energy and pull in new results. Create our desires in our hearts and take action to secure them by taking the first step toward them.

I have a quote that urges me to get on with the rest of my life:-

> *"I have a sense of destiny that won't allow me to die with my music still in me".*

Wayne Dyer, The Power of Intention.

It's time to step back and realise we are not the person we have come to know, but a Spirit much grander. It is time to let that other person go and embrace the new. Armed with a new attitude and outlook, it's time to create through action. It is amazing how many situations can be resolved simply by taking action on a change in attitude.

We need to get into a space where we are satisfied with our purpose in life. I am talking about satisfying our Spirit in the purpose that we choose. Spirit feels no satisfaction in the acquisition of things. Strong heartfelt action can bring us the results we desire – it all involves the focusing of energy. I prefer to seek the deeper feeling of satisfaction that comes when my soul is singing.

As we go into action, let Spirit be our guide. We establish intentions for ourselves and go into action while consciously being aware that we have a partner more knowledgeable than our own conscious being. So recognize it as a partnership and be alert for intuition to guide us in our life. Spirit is a gentle guide with a gentle signal, hence the need for calmness in our Be-ing. The feeling of Spirit comes from around our solar plexus, hence the expression "a gut feeling." If we hear a voice from between our ears I suggest we may be hearing from our ego. Once we have decided on something and have a clear vision, let Spirit take over, and if we can, do something to help the vision happen. We alone prevent Spirit from partnering up with us.

It is not that we have been denied this connection all our lives. We each have had many experiences and at times have known they involved Spirit. We have also experienced a wide range of feelings, so this is about spending more time experiencing the best of these: joy, a sense of inner peace, and a deep satisfaction with life, however simple it may be.

We embrace our power and allow Spirit to guide us to what it wishes for us, rather than what we wish for ourselves. This requires a lot of faith. I cannot imagine going forward without this sense of having an ally. There is a transition that feels like we are losing control until we realize how much better it feels to have Spirit involved. Once connected, we realize we are still in control, but in a much more powerful and satisfying way.

Your point of power is in the present moment. Now! You, and you alone, are the power in your life. This is the moment in which we can engage our Spiritual power and walk side by side with Spirit. When we react to what is going on around us with emotion we surrender our power, we become vulnerable to all sorts of energy flows and invasions. Our reaction to a situation tells us whether we are coming from Spirit or ego, and if we are emotional then it is ego at work. The love flowing from Spirit has no attachment to outcome and is therefore at ease with the moment.

When we turn to the mind for change we turn to the point of opportunity. The ego loves to manage our mind, so it is always looking to influence the outcome of our visit to our mind. It is through managing our mind that we start a new thought process, so we need to be fully aware that we are in charge of the moment and that we are not running our thoughts through the filter of the ego. Basically, the ego seeks to maintain the status quo and our Spirit seeks change, so there is potential conflict.

Once we have a new thought about something or a situation it is time to create a new image of what we desire. We need to see the outcome clearly and whenever our thought processes comes back to the subject then we need to have the same image in front of our mind, without wavering, or we blur the image and risk mixed results.

When the image is clear and we feel good inside about our intention, accept it as a *fait accompli*. Now, right now. There is only this moment. We cannot defer to the future, for that is then where we are inviting our image to be – always in the future. Now is now, future is future – they never align. We confidently wait until the mailman comes. In the meantime, Spirit is not only seeking to serve us, it can actually refine the outcome to make it even better, because we have kept our energy off of the outcome. Whatever Spirit brings to us is for our utmost benefit in this moment.

If there is a maybe, then there is doubt, and the outcome is in jeopardy.

However, when we are giving up our feeling of control over the outcome, some homework may be necessary before we can clear the path to feeling open to surrender. Start moving toward our objectives and let Spirit unveil the details as we move forward. We will be moving toward a great sense of freedom. In the world of Spirit there is only "now time." When we state our intention we assume it is so. We do not expect it to occur in the future after certain other events have taken place. Action is important, but detailed planning beyond the next step in a way denies the power of Spirit. We may be focusing our mental energies in a direction that Spirit does not want to go and Spirit now needs to get past our energy to guide us. The vision of intention should be clear, but held loosely.

Intention

Every day is the first day of the rest of your life. It does not matter what has gone before, you can make a fresh start today. Running your life has a lot of similarities to running a business. Clear intentions set management by objective. The intentions can cover several fields. Take a look at yourself and decide on the changes you choose just for yourself, to improve your own life. A new you could include healthier eating, exercise, and more recreation time. You show love for yourself when you carry through on these intentions. Establish how you choose to project yourself into your surrounding world. How would you like to be creative? What sort of results would have you feeling pleased with your efforts? How do you plan to connect with your Spirit more often and harness your senior partner's power? Do you wish to change the way you interact with those around you at home, at work or at play? Then there is the material world, about which we often say derogatory things. If the couch is falling apart, how about a new one? If you love watching a lot of TV, would you enjoy it more on a larger screen? You can always give the other one away. We in the western world have created a society in which we have these choices and sometimes it is nice to acquire some accessories. Buying accessories can be pleasurable, as long it does not become obsessive. We do need material things to function in our society; it is our attitude to the acquisition that is important.

How do we determine what to tackle first? Usually we take on the item that is uppermost in life right now, the one that is grabbing our attention. There might be something that we feel is important to resolve before anything else. We are individuals; each of us is unique and so our responses are also unique. We create our own to-do list. Visualise the outcome you desire and then let it go over to your Spirit. If a series of actions are required on your part, start the ball rolling. Do not plan too far in advance; hold the details loosely so that Spirit can also play with them. Such a relaxed approach can only lead to a superior outcome.

So remember, create the intention, the image, and have no attachment to outcome. In that way you turn your intention over to your Spirit. Go into action as required.

Our intention for life does not have to entail lofty goals. It only needs goals whose accomplishment satisfy us, that nourish our soul. Once intention is in place, move toward those goals with passion and live in the moment with vitality. Perseverance and determination keep energy focused, which helps move us toward the completion of our intention. On the other hand, do not become so focused that you become that rock in the river, unavailable for help from your own Spirit. It is a balancing act. You need some grit to get through.

> *"Genius is one percent inspiration and ninety-nine percent perspiration"*
>
> – Thomas Edison
>
> *"Persistence alone is omnipotent"*
>
> – Leland Val Van DeWall

Choose who you desire to be, how you desire to express, and be comfortable with whom you have chosen to be. When results are not what are expected, first look in the mirror of your own personal experience for change, not to the outside world. At times, when you miss acting in accordance with your intention, go easy on yourself. Let go, recharge, and move forward.

Act as if your intention is already achieved – you are just awaiting confirmation. Be persistent and keep building momentum and energy. No wavering, having second thoughts is inviting mixed results.

Trust in the process, stay in the moment, and always love yourself. The key is in the "now moment", being enthusiastic about participation in this moment, in other words, living. And if nothing seems to be going on it is time to meditate on what is happening – the leaf on the tree, the bird flitting between the branches, the new shoot emerging from the ground, the person walking the dog, your own breathing. Marvel at the world around you, express and feel gratitude several times a day.

Focus

Once you have set an intention for yourself pursue it with a single-mindedness that does not waiver. Stay focused. Be determined to stay the course. Never contemplate the absence of what you seek, for it will delay its arrival temporarily or even permanently. Watch out for the times when you focus on what is missing in your life. Switch to gratitude for what you do have.

The moment we lose focus and let our thoughts digress we create another picture for the Universe and it will adjust to our new energy and attempt to satisfy our new direction. When we keep vacillating about our intention, when we have doubt about the outcome, we create another vibration to be accommodated and the outcome is therefore now in doubt. We are giving out mixed signals and muddled minds create muddled results. We cannot keep changing our minds; the Universe is doing its best to keep up. Mind, body, and Spirit need to be united in purpose and focus. Avoid having a Plan B. That is something so many of us have, a fall-back plan. It works against us because it creates a secondary intention, a mixed message. Go full ahead with Plan A until you succeed or hit a brick wall and have to reconsider where you have erred in harnessing and focusing your energy.

The Universe is our faithful servant. It is serving us exactly what we are asking for, so if we do not like what is on the menu today make a change, and this time become more focused. There can be no "what if." And so it is.

Listening to our feelings will help us stay focused. If we feel uneasy about something, ask a question or two and be alert for the response. Does all this sound too complicated? It does not have to be. It feels this way because the human race has created a complicated scenario and there is so much "stuff" going on, so many differing and negative energies going around, it is difficult to stay in balance and harmony. Is it all worth the effort? Yes it is. It becomes easier and as it does, so confidence increases, and then we are on our way. I believe in the KIS (keep it simple) principle, and life is simple when we align with our inner self. The complicated part is figuring out how to connect with ourselves consistently and that is what we are contemplating right now. Ask yourself if you are coming from a place of love and compassion.

"What would love do now" – Neale Donald Walsch, Conversations with God, Book One

We must become a keen observers of life so that we can make adjustments to remain focused. Answers are always within. If we catch ourselves focusing on an event, person, or relationship outside of ourselves, get centred and go within. Speak when spoken to. We were given two ears and one mouth and that should tell us something. When we give advice without invitation, it will draw us toward the energy and experience of that other person. Invite them to create their own solution by asking questions that encourage them to create their own information. In this way we are not invading their space and their energy. We are showing respect and at the same time we are attempting to help. This will help keep us focused on our own life. Support someone else, never try and do for someone else.

When we want to re-focus and get back into now time just ask the questions. What time is it – now. What am I doing with my time now – and that will cause you to focus on where your mind is at this moment and you can spot the error and bring focus to the moment.

Non-attachment

This is a key, in my opinion, for harnessing the power of our Spiritual Be-ing. We remove mindful expectation by not having any attachment to the outcome of any situation. When we remove mindful expectation from a situation we have no concern for the possible outcomes. This removes fear from the situation, and with fear out of the picture, love is free to flow. Love is our Spirit, free to express. Spirit is free to guide us, nourish us, and seek our highest good. Mindful expectation is associated with ego and is to be differentiated from the expectation that goes with Spiritual creation. With Spiritual creation there is an assumption of an outcome born out of faith in our ability to create. However, there is no attachment to that outcome – we leave the details to our Spirit partner and trust the outcome is the best for our journey.

I know of no other aspect that produces faster results. I acknowledge that people who have a goal and pursue it with determination and a positive attitude invariably bring about the desired goal. Energy flows to where the concentration goes and creates. That is human endeavour. I say, better still, get out of the way and let Spirit join the show. It's a bit like comparing a bicycle to a BMW. Action is invariably needed to support our intention, but not a forceful attitude. Forcing an outcome creates a lot of negative energy and disruption along the path to realisation.

Be patient with life, for things are not always what they appear. There is a story of a young man working on a farm during the American Civil War. He broke his leg just before harvest. A neighbour came by and said to his father what a hardship it was to have the boy unable to help with the harvest. To which the father replied, "We'll see."

A week later the army came through the village seizing recruits for the war. They passed on the boy because of his broken leg. Now the neighbour was saying what a blessing it was that the boy broke his leg. "We'll see," said the father. And so the story continued.

Life is not about success as much of the western world defines it. It is about letting go and being you, this will allow Spirit to bring on success, probably in a form that you had not imagined and yet is even more satisfying than you had ever dreamed.

We have practiced bringing things into our lives and maybe not recognized it. This does not have to be about big things. I can invariably produce a parking spot in the centre of our crazy city that is so desperate for downtown parking. I just have that expectation. I do not contemplate the possibilities of not getting space. I have no fear attached to whether or not I get one, so I usually do. I think we know what happens if we are late and conscious of it – we probably hit a bunch of red lights, road works, and of course my usual convenient parking spot would not be available to me and I would have to go round the block three times, except there is a one way street in there that turns it into a three-block trip. Do you know the feeling? Then bring it on into the mainstream of your life, the positive "don't have an attachment" feeling and apply it to the important things in your life. The feeling and the principle is the same whatever the subject.

Action

Next we decide how we are going to back up our intention with some action. Or, maybe it is something we have to wait to come about, so we are patient, but not so patient that the whole idea stagnates. We must learn to accept that what we desire in our lives is already so, and not to expect it to occur in the future after certain other events have taken place. Action is important, but detailed planning can deny the power that is. That is what the mind can do for you. It is our human input centre, beyond which we hand off to our Spiritual centre for fine-tuning and completion.

Affirmations, as outlined in Chapter 10, can help with our focus. State intentions clearly and in the present tense. "I am" is the most powerful way to start an affirmation, so if this start for the affirmation fits, please use it. Absolutely avoid using words like "want" and "try," and any negative word like "not" or "never." Always make a positive statement and stay in the present tense.

We can apply our images and affirmations to all the situations in our lives, relationships, vocations and vacations, material things, and, of course, healing our pain through compassion, forgiveness, and love. If we cannot identify the things from the past that lead to our present circumstances, then focus on our own self-image. Build yourself up; be happy and proud of who you are, the principles you stand for, and how you express yourself. All this is work that is done in "now time" and is so powerful.

A statement like, "I am not going to smoke, starting tomorrow" or "I am going to stop smoking tomorrow" have no power. In both cases they are not really statements of intent because they talk of tomorrow. These statements cannot be repeated for more than one day before becoming obsolete. The subconscious does not recognize the negative in the first one so this changes the statement in the first example to "I am (not) going to smoke starting tomorrow." Actually it is the verb smoke that is creating the image and the image is about smoking. Focus on the new image of yourself; avoid all reference to the old.

"I breathe fresh air all the time" creates a different picture. Once we are really comfortable with our choice of words, add some spice to the words and say them with passion. Repeat them over and over, whenever you get the chance, even under your breath. And have an image to go with the affirmation. In this case an image could be you on top of a mountain breathing the fresh air. Ignore the cigarette ad that wants us on top of a mountain with a smile on our face, a lovely partner at our side, and both of us puffing away. Another powerful reinforcement is to look into our eyes in front of a mirror and affirm it there.

You can pick up a book of affirmations if you feel uncertain about creating your own. I suggest you adjust those that you find that do not follow the guidelines I have suggested for negativity and word choice. Not all writers apply these guidelines and I believe they are vitally important.

Reminders

Remember to treat yourself well and as if you are worthwhile. If you truly think you are worthwhile you would set aside time for yourself and your interests, and when you choose to set aside this time you will affirm yourself as worth the effort.

Energy
Remember that energy flows to where the concentration goes. This applies whether the energy is focused on thoughts or actions. To think to the past keeps it alive, but only in the mind, nowhere else. While we are in the past we are not

living in the present moment. However, we need time to create by dreaming about the future without slipping into a fantasyland.

The wise person focuses on what is going on inside. We take care of our own energy and stay out of the energy of others.

Ask and you shall receive, and as the Universe hears from you so it responds. We do not always understand that we are sending mixed messages. One prime area of error already mentioned is wanting. The word stands for lack. So the Universe delivers more of the same. We have to choose our thoughts and actions carefully, for the Universe is a faithful and obedient servant. Today's results are a result of past thoughts and actions. Today we prepare for tomorrow. Today well lived makes for a great tomorrow.

Enjoy and embrace the journey; goals happen and it's better to enjoy Spirit's goals than those we create in our own mind. Wherever we arrive we are fulfilling a goal set either by our humanity or by Spirit. Our present circumstances reflect our past plans, whether we were conscious of them or not. The energy we projected in the past has come home to roost. Today's energy sets up tomorrow.

Observe

Instead of judging learn to observe. Be the angel in your world and look down on what is happening. Avoid slipping over into judgement by keeping on the observation side of the line. This requires that we have no emotional attachment to what we observe. We observe a person's actions. We can choose to like or dislike what they are doing; however, we must stop short of judging them for what they do or judgement will surely be visited back on us, sooner or later. It must happen, because you have given the "picture" energy and it will expand and return to you. Separate the act from the person, for behind every person is Spirit, the same Spirit that dwells in you.

Pay attention to what is going on with our new intention, keep our awareness high and we can stay in control, for awareness and ego cannot co-exist. Stay in the moment and out of the past or future, for the latter two rob you of time and life passes us by because we have moved to a dead space.

Flow

Life is like a river; it flows. Trying to be a rock in the river and forcing the water of life to flow around does not work. Worse still, trying to swim upstream against the current does not work – it invites disaster. Some results take perseverance and determination. However, when we feel we are being pushed back hard it may call for a change of direction. It is for us to feel the difference and flow with life. I have pushed hard for an outcome that went against the flow of events that were unfolding easily in my life. I forced an issue that changed my life, and the result was a very difficult time in my life. I did not understand then what I know now. Force invariably creates disappointing results.

So let us go with the flow, keep fear out of the way, and have no attachment to the outcome. When we can embrace this concept and put it into practice results will fly back to us.

This, I find, is a difficult concept to put into words because it is something to be experienced in order to be fully understood. If you do not fully grasp it now stick with it; this concept is powerful.

The results we see today are a perfect reflection of the energy we were expressing yesterday and in the days and months before that. It is a perfect checklist for where we were at in the past. If we do not like what we observe, then we fix it. How? First we write down a list of the things that grab our attention. Then we write a list of how we would like them to be. A third list describes the differences between the two and this will give us a list of our erroneous zones that still need healing. There is a belief to which we are still giving energy that creates each difference that we list. Focus on the difference, bring it into awareness, and make its healing one of our intentions. Go within!

Freedom and control

As our walk with Spirit becomes closer, so our sense of freedom will grow. Our freedom will depend on how much responsibility we assume for our life, how much we put ourselves in control, rather than letting control slip away so that someone else is influencing how we run our life.

Control starts by acknowledging our point of power is now. It involves being in charge of our current thought, what is going on in our mind. Going through our mind is a necessary avenue toward change. It is our place of conscious control and when we go there we need to be ready to engage our ego, for it likes to control our mind. We must be the masters of our mind. Either we are in control of our life and our choices, or someone or something else is in control. Manage your energy – never give it away. It will slip away at times, so be alert and ready to reclaim it.

Gratitude

Live with gratitude for what you have. Focusing on gratitude will cause it to expand. Every morning I get up and turn on the tap and water comes out and I am full of gratitude. What a blessing, and what's more the water is drinkable and the daily cost for availability is low. Now we just need to bring this wonderful blessing to the billions that do not have it.

The high road
It makes for a better sleep if we choose the high road in any situation – what we believe to be the honourable thing to do in the circumstances. Let us be led by our conscience and feel in harmony, regardless of what others are saying. To do otherwise puts energy into the low road and its consequences. Whatever we visit on another is a statement about what we choose for ourselves and the faithful Universe will eventually return it to us, usually multiplied. Our gift to another is a gift to ourselves, so we need to be careful what we give away by virtue of words and actions.

Abundance and giving
If we are, or become, abundant in material wealth, keep it moving. It tells the Universe we feel we have enough to share; keeping wealth moving unconsciously declares that we expect to have enough for ourselves because we are passing it on. The idea is to not hang on, but circulate our blessings, and help others to their feet so that they can be independent. And if they, for some reason, cannot function independently, then just give graciously. That means giving without any expectation of receiving anything back from the recipient or the Universe. It is time to have a faith in the Universe that it will always provide for our good, without specific expectation.

In the process of giving always remember to include yourself. Give yourself the time to do things that you enjoy so that you can nourish yourself and have your strength renewed. Without your strength you have little to offer, so it is not selfish to put yourself first. It is easier to give from strength.

Hazards and roadblocks

The heading makes it sound as if we are heading into a bunch of road works. When we are driving and we do come to road works we have to be particularly alert. And so it is with guiding our life, there are obstacles that need to be heeded. We have been feeding energy to some of our beliefs for decades and ego is reluctant to let go. So what do we watch for that might derail us or tell us that we are not on track?

Anger
Anger is one of the biggest things we do to cover up our desire not to change. It is a sign we do not want to look at something. And be alert for its little siblings, criticism and irritability. Another particular concern with anger is that it is expressed, or suppressed, with a lot of emotion. There is a lot of energy concentrated making whatever image we have, at that moment of expression, very powerful. Better to use that energy at the time we do our affirmations. See yourself at peace when you feel anger rising.

Many of us still struggle with anger. It gets in the way of healing and feeling in a big way. Our early applications of compassion, forgiveness, and love would be well applied around issues that bring up anger. Remember, we own our emotions and nobody can make you angry without your consent. Anger is fear announced. When we have nothing to fear, we have nothing over which to be angry. The idea is we are not angry when we don't get what we want, because our wanting it was simply a preference, not a necessity.

Now, having said all that, there are situations that stir my emotions and I feel anger, for example, any form of child abuse.

Judgement

I touch on it yet again. Stay away from it, for it will take us down an unpleasant path and we in turn will find ourselves judged. How do you react to panhandlers? Yes, they may well be professionals (there is a school for panhandlers), and they may be better dressed than expected. To anticipate how they are going to spend our gift is a judgment. This is not about giving if there is judgment, it is about us, but then it is always about us. Are we giving to life or are we judging life? I think this is one of the greatest scenarios for checking out where we are at and for understanding the principles involved. We need to be aware of where we are at in any given moment so that we can express the best of ourselves. So what will happen next time you meet up with a panhandler? And consider this – it is not for us to understand another's journey or even attempt to do so. The quickest way to salvation for a soul may be through the dark alley of who they are not, and by withholding our gift this day we may have denied the panhandler the money needed for the bottle that was going to push him to the bottom of his world, from where he would make a stand and start healing. Many of us have to hit "bottom" before we start a determined road to recovery. Do not let our judgment get in the way lest you deny another his golden opportunity. We do not know of the mysteries that are being weaved beyond our understanding. Give into this world to the extent that it feels good. Judgement never feels good. It is time to leave judgment behind. No, there are no exceptions. Judgment requires our energy to pursue a non-loving direction. Whatever energy we put out must come back to us. Judge and be judged!

Criticism
Criticism is a warning signal suggesting unfinished business. In effect, we are offering judgment. We also need to check whether we are criticizing the person, or their personality as expressed in their actions. We are One, so when we criticize another we are in effect pointing a finger at ourselves. The words we use to criticize anyone or anything indicates the manner of criticism we harbour for ourselves.

Complaining
Complaining is one of the worst aspects of mind chatter. Whether the words are spoken or just running through our mind; they are robbing us of our presence in the now moment. We complain about the weather, traffic, transit, our job, our boss. We wish and want for things, in other words, we are complaining about the status quo and showing dissatisfaction for our blessings. When someone is kind enough to ask how we are, sometimes our response is, "Oh, it's Monday," or "I would feel better if the weather was better." We get so caught up in complaining we don't actually listen to the question. The person was asking how we are; they were not asking about which day it is or the weather. I am sure you have heard people talk this way. When in this mood we are totally out of the moment. At these times we block Spirit from coming through. We cannot be happy, let alone joyous. We are transmitting a general negative energy and it will pull in anything else close by that is on a similar wavelength, and we end up with more about which to complain. This mood keeps us trapped in no man's land, ego-land. Watch the "mind chatter" and be aware of the words that come out of our mouths.

Digging into the past

Digging into the past in order to heal without clues from the present is not a wise move. We can get lost in analysis. It is enough to identify through the clues of the present day mirror those things we need to review and then heal. There are times when we need to go back for review, but it is not a starting point, as if we are on a witch hunt to heal all the past right now. Current circumstances will tell us in which order we need to proceed.

Ego

I refer often to the ego. There will be times when it just does not seem to want to give up its power over something – it sticks around like a pesky mosquito as we lie in bed in the dark. Be prepared to manage the ego in such circumstances. Recognise when it tries to take over and have a planned reaction.

Stay out of the negative side of the past; in fact stay out of any negative conversation or thought. Now, that is a tall order with all that is going on in the world; we need to observe the difficulties and talk solutions. In a similar manner, we need to do the same with our own smaller world. The past also includes this morning. Stop vacillating and keep your mind constant, always looking in the direction you intend to travel.

Pain

Benjamin Franklin said, *"Those things that hurt instruct."* This is provided we recognize the opportunity and give it a chance. Pain is our signpost; working through it will give us freedom. Our ego is closely associated with the pain body we have accumulated, so when our pain is triggered it is a good time to take stock and reveal what is coming up for healing.

Worrying

Dutch author Corrie ten Boom said in Clippings from My Notebook, *"Worrying does not empty tomorrow of its sorrow, it empties today of its strength."*

Worrying never, ever, solved anything. It is a total waste of time and energy. The energy creates visions, usually negative, which disturb our bodies and impair our immune system. I cannot think of another aspect of living that delivers a more definitive zero and that is why the subject is brought up yet again.

Fear

Fear is the messenger that tells us that we need to heal. When we are gripped by fear, to any degree, it is time to look at the subject at hand, because trying to push through without emotional healing denies us the opportunity for an optimal outcome.

Wanting

Wanting is just another way of reminding ourselves that we do not have something. We are lamenting about something that it is not in our lives at this moment and consequently our sub-conscious acts on that feeling of absence and we continue to go without, because that is what we have really chosen for ourselves. "I am" and "I intend" have immensely more power as statements than "I want."

Avoidance

Avoidance and procrastination come in many forms. There are addictions to drugs, alcohol, smoking, working, and gambling. Then there is anger, procrastination, or "being too busy." They all give us time-wasting techniques that tell the observer that we do not want to deal with the nagging pain inside.

American psychologist William James stated, *"Nothing is so fatiguing as the hanging on of an uncompleted task."*

Another anonymous quote cuts to the chase: *"Procrastination is the flab of an undisciplined mind."*

Force

Force negates growth. We need the confidence to plant our seeds and water our garden in the knowledge that what we sow we shall reap. Do not do as the little boy once did – pull the plants out of the ground to see how they were doing. Sow with confidence. Force will focus energy toward a preconceived outcome and, given enough energy, we will surely make progress in that direction. Force invites fear into the picture because we now have attachment to the outcome. The presence of fear is never in our best interest.

Unfinished business

When I harp on past experiences the message is I am not finished with the experience, I have more to learn, and I am re-energizing the subject. It is a drain on my energy until it is resolved, so it is beneficial to engage the energy necessary to move through the old experience.

Our negative feelings will give past experiences energy and they will linger and take up more of our time. Just observe and move on with the day, for this too will pass.

Reaction

The more emotionally reactive we are, the more we will become involved in the outer world, and the longer we stay embroiled in the outer world, the more challenging life will seem. Once we shift outside of ourselves we step into the playground not only of our own ego, but also the egos of others. We are then tangled with their energy. It is important to maintain a calm attitude to what is going on around us and be unaffected by potential outcomes.

Physical world

Our physical world is unpredictable; however, we need to know ourselves well enough that we respond with ease to what is going on around us. If we are not at ease then we need to engage our mind and change our attitude. I admit I struggle with this aspect of life with all that I see of man's inhumanity to man, the lack of adequate world community, and widespread starvation, corruption, greed, and desire for power.

Reputation

There is a book called *What You Think of Me is None of My Business* by Whittaker Cole. I have not read the book, but there is a message in the title that is poignant. I heard Wayne Dyer talk about reputation. He said that if he is addressing 3,000 people, then at the end of the evening he has 3,000 reputations out there based on the filters applied by the individuals in the audience. They will vary from high praise to the totally dissatisfied. This is despite all 3,000 hearing the same words. You can only be yourself. To seek a certain reputation in the minds of others is to put yourself on a treadmill you will never get off. You only need to be satisfied with yourself and your own performance. When you are concerned about your reputation you are giving your power away to the other person or persons.

Questioning a situation

Be careful what and how you question what is going on. Often times our power lies in accepting what is. To question something oftentimes suggests something is missing, that something is wrong, that there is a lack of something. It is better not to focus on lack.

Give and be open to receive

In the act of giving we declare we have enough and the Universe fulfills that declaration by replacing what we give away. As a salesperson I can go out to just get a sale to help fill my quota or I can go to the customer and sell him something that I know will serve his needs. Do I focus on giving service or getting what I think I need? I have been in many sales meetings where the emphasis has been on meeting quotas. In one of my vocations I had access to the private areas of a major bank. I could not help noticing the colourful advertisement on the staff notice board for a trip to Jamaica for the staff member who sold the most of a particular investment instrument. It struck me that a large number of customers could end up with less than an optimum investment portfolio because of over-zealous sales staff seeking a free trip. As we give so we receive; be aware of the karma you are creating for yourself.

Expectation

I expect you to do your best, although your best may be more or less than my best, and vice versa; the effort, or lack thereof, is for each to address.

Remove expectations from others. There will be situations where the actions of others will not meet tolerable levels of behaviour, at which time intervention is necessary, as in the case of abuse, violence or other breach of the law. That is not to say the law is perfect. That is why we keep changing the laws and different countries have different expectations of their citizens expressed in their laws.

However, in non-violent and non-abusive situations, remove expectation, for it is a judgement. Be prepared instead to offer encouragement and compassion.

There is much to consider if we are to make improvements in our lives. Just sitting around thinking about life will not change much, so I wish you an exciting journey of action.

Chapter 13

Communication

Communicate with the inner self first

*T*he first level of communication is with self, that is, our inner self. The better connected we are to Spirit, the better we can communicate in life and move toward our objectives. Spirit is our most important level of communication. Our lives revolve around our own performance and knowing ourselves, then taking that knowledge and using it to express the best of ourselves in the outer world. We need to make good choices for ourselves and in order to do that we need to develop ourselves, and so it follows we need to understand ourselves. We need to be able to sit quietly and get to know the person that we are. The alternative is to run around living life at the bidding of the ego. Another reason for good communication with self is that all the answers lie within; only clues lie outside of us. We need to be able to integrate these two areas of our lives.

A strong link with Spirit gives us a strong link to the Power of the Universe, which is at our disposal. Spirit not only gives us a beautiful sense of inner peace, but also helps us so much in the world around us as we express that sense of inner peace wherever we go. Spirit influences the world around us and the results we draw to ourselves.

Then communicate with others

Once we establish a good relationship with ourselves, our new vibration will affect the relationships around us in different ways. Some people will drop out of our lives quietly and others will offer some resistance as they attempt to keep us in their lives without change.

This represents a challenge and we need to honour ourselves as things change. This will be a bigger challenge when the change involves close family. Walk the high road and allow things to unfold. Stay focused on your commitment to yourself.

We need to remember that when we have a breakthrough in our growth that it is not a time to go out and try converting people to our new way of being. Just let our example speak for itself and people will ask if they are interested. The people who want to share your new wisdom will identify themselves.

We assert ourselves with calm and dignity. Allow others to follow their own path, even if they do not appear to be making wise choices. It is not for us to understand the journey of another.

The response of others should not rule our decisions. It is our reaction that is all-important. We may end up accepting that they are offering us wisdom, or that there is wisdom to be gleaned from the interaction we are experiencing.

Whatever the situation, we are responsible for our own journey and that is why we need to get to know ourselves as a top priority. Our interaction with others gives us a mirror in which to reflect. Our reaction is our choice and the key to our own growth.

If you would like to see a change in your circumstances, go within and ensure that you are in harmony with your desired intention. You run your life, so make sure you know yourself well.

Always communicate without attachment to the outcome – there is that important statement once again.

Chapter 14

Love

The truth – that love is the ultimate and the highest goal to which Man can aspire.

– Viktor Frankl, Experiences in a Concentration Camp

What is love?

The word love is right up there amongst the most attention-getting words on the planet. The answer to understanding love is to be found in our hearts by connecting to our Spirit. Hopefully, some of the thoughts in this chapter will help you on your journey, and I am sure readers have some interesting opinions of their own.

We know by now that we are Spirit. When we are able to peel back all the layers of our humanity and experience who we truly are we will discover that all there is, is love. Our Creator has created a Universe that is Love. The only thing on this planet that gets in the way of the flow of love is our humanity.

Love is all there is to our Spirit. Love is the only reality. We create everything else, and much of what we create interferes with the flow of love. Release our overlapping creations and we get to experience the flow of true love. We will discover that love asks for no_thing. We are love and love is always with us. If we are not feeling fully embraced by love then it is ours to rediscover. I say rediscover because love is who we are, as Spirit. We are just experiencing some disconnect.

Love starts and finishes with you. If you feel disconnected from the feeling of love, or have any sort of yearning, seek to love yourself, as you are, today, in this moment. You are love. You need to put yourself first among the list of people you love. Hold love in your Be-ing, for being "in love" with someone or something else is not enough.

Many years ago I read *The Seat of the Soul* by Gary Zugov. The very clear message I gained from the book was there are one of two places to be, we are either coming from a place of love, or from a place of fear. Fear sits in opposition to love, it not hate. Hate is not the opposite of love, it is the absence of love.

Love flows easily, fear grips and holds on. Love asks no questions, it exists in total acceptance. Fear asks questions and manipulates. In order to release our fearful emotions we need to introduce the healing light of love.

Emotions are born of fear, and feeling emotional about love is often mistaken for an expression of love or being "in love." For some of us that is the only kind of loving experience we have had. We mistake it for the real thing. Love is blissful, it is not a giddy emotion, and love is the light that transcends fearful emotion.

Love is, and yet that is not what we have necessarily learned about love. We learned as we grew up, through our interaction with parents, siblings, relatives and other experiences in life, that love is conditional. There is so much withholding in the human experience. We are asked so often to "do" in order to receive. Remember that our parents were not trained in parenting. We do not go to school to learn about the most important job on earth.

Experiencing unconditional love is a wonderful goal in life and will set you free once you experience it. Your ego will lose its power, it will still be there, but you will be in control, and from your loving position as an unconditional observer you will strike an easy balance.

The moment we introduce any sort of judgement to a situation or are attached to the outcome we have lost our connection. Our position has slipped to a conditional one, which is not love at all.

When we call in love to any situation we set fear aside. Trusting that love will prevail is a challenge, for some circumstances defy a solution based on intellectual input. Faith will prevail if you can truly step back and allow love to flow. Love is, in all cases, unconditional, and our outlook needs to be the same to avoid a blockage to this connection.

Once we connect with love we can heal with love. We can either focus on going within and finding the love that is there, to find that blissful inner peace, or, alternatively, we can go outside of ourselves and use the mirror of life to heal and eventually discover the love within. The more likely route is to attempt both simultaneously.

Let it be, with love. Love cures all. As I have said, all pain is learned – it came from someone else's pain.

Aspects of love

Love is disciplined. Discipline toward self is a demonstration of love. Discipline in how we treat others is a sign of love. Lead another by example – do not do for another. Do not attempt to take responsibility for the life of another – it is theirs to lead.

Our natural state is one of joy. Like love, joy is enduring. Happiness is something we experience, primarily through letting go of unhappiness. It is like everything else, clean house, put out the garbage, and we are left with what is meaningful. Nobody else can be responsible for our happiness but ourselves. Someone can add to our happiness by being in our life, but only we can elect to be happy. This is so important in relationships; the other person is not there to make us happy, they are there to share our life.

Love is a celebration. When we are connected to that loving feeling we add greatly to life around us. We bring the best of us to any situation and our shining light will help inspire others. Our unique approach to life is a gift to share.

Love is a state of non-separation. We separate when we focus on and believe something or someone outside of us holds the key to love and joy in our life. In other words, when we believe in our ego's perception of life we separate ourselves from love.

Also, love can only exist in a state of non-attachment to outcome. Only then can love be free for guidance from our Spirit. If you have read this before it is because this concept has been mentioned several times previously in this book. That is how important it is to our expression of love, of the expression of our true Be-ing.

Love survives the passage of time because it is the ultimate power in the Universe. Have you noticed that, in most cases, with the passage of time your memory of past events and relationships usually comes around more to the positive? It is because the negative is based in the ego and it needs to feed on your energy in order to survive. Love flows from an infinite source and keeps no record of wrong. When we put events out of our mind for a while then the ego base fades gradually into oblivion. If we are able to maintain a strong emotional attachment to past events, and they keep coming up in our mind, a healing is needed. Maybe it is time to see a professional.

I see love as the glue that holds a relationship together in difficult times. Love is the core feeling that we have for another that hangs in there when the going gets tough, while we get those egocentric interruptions out of the way.

And so it is that we take our connection to Spirit, to the ever-present love that flows, and let it bring out the best in us. We strive, with Spirit's help, to be the best we can be in any given situation, on any day. When we falter, we dust ourselves off, forgive ourselves for our mistake, and forge on in the only time there is – this moment. To dwell on the past takes us back to a vision that does not exist, except in our minds. We can only keep the past in our minds if we insist on using energy to keep the vision there.

The absence of real love in our lives often comes from accepting from our past experiences that we are not good enough. We have learned that from outside of ourselves, but love is not to be found outside – there is only the celebration of the love within. There is a sense of love that is illusionary, that feels exciting and feels like you have arrived. It is present when ego connects in vibration. Two people seeking love to nourish themselves find each other, the vibration connects. It feels good, but it is in fact two half people seeking to make a whole. Two halves are always two halves because we are individuals and, as much as we may try and lose ourselves in another, it cannot happen at the Spiritual level. Two whole people coming together in love do not make one either – they remain as two individuals choosing to express their love together in harmony. We need to stop pursuing love through the auspices of the ego. Ego wants nothing to do with true love, for it spells the death knell of the ego. Love heals fear, the basis for the destructive side of the ego.

And therein lies the dichotomy of life. The struggle to have love heal fear and override the pain expressed through ego. Ego seeks to keep us off balance so that we cannot experience love. Ego presents as fear, the very opposite of love.

Relationships

Love is not to be found in a relationship, just as we cannot find anything else by looking outside of ourselves. Love is found within. Partnerships are for expressing love, sharing love. Our partner can give love, but cannot replace the love that we may feel is missing. That is because it is always their love, their gift to you. It cannot replace a hole in your heart. Only you can do the repair work.

Many of us have placed expectations on our partner that, in reality, they cannot fulfill. These expectations are based on what we have learned. When we are disappointed that we have not received what we expect, then resentment creeps in and starts to fester. It drives a wedge between two people.

A partnership needs to recognize that it is a Spiritual partnership brought together so that we may each support the other in the journey through life. We are together because we enjoy each other and feel each other are worthy of love. However, the other person is not going to fix us or fill the voids in our life or our hearts. They can only support us in our own efforts. A relationship is about two individuals.

Never, ever compromise in a relationship. Compromise is a concept of a relationship that has been passed down through the ages. Compromise eventually results in resentment, which will eventually destroy a relationship, even if a couple loves each other. Love struggles if it is asked to betray itself. In place of compromise, seek co-operation with each other. If agreement cannot be reached, then let it be and honour the individuality in your partner. Quickly let go of the disappointment.

Keep ego out of relationships. That includes any attempt to control the thoughts and actions of a partner. If we observe our partner doing something born of their ego rather than their Spirit, keep it as an observation and stay out of judgement. A few well-chosen comments are what friendships are built around.

If there is an addiction present in the relationship then the addict is declaring they have a lot of pain they are trying to cover up. The suppression of the pain can be so important that the addiction is more important than the relationship. We end up playing second fiddle to the addiction and therefore cannot reach our potential, as a couple. Such triangles do not work. It is difficult to stay out of judgement in such situations. Once again, we must be the observer and not the judge. Creating an intervention is a loving and gutsy thing to do.

When we are able to shine and give our best we contribute to the world. Every contribution is important. In one sense one person amongst over seven billion on this planet seems insignificant. However, if a billion people shift in a positive direction it will be felt immensely on this planet. We must show up and vote and together we can make a difference.

There are millions of people out there showing us the way, doing wonderful work to improve the lot of their fellow men and to preserve the environment. They need and deserve the support of the billions. Please offer your loving and practical support.

Loving yourself means getting out of bed with the intention of being the best person you can be. In this way you honour yourself and create hope for the future. May your future shine in the Light of Love.

Finis

Acknowledgements

I wish to thank Judy Hughes for her wise input and generous amount of time she devoted to editing this book as it progressed through about a dozen drafts over several years on its way to publication.

To Andrea Steell for her enthusiastic support, for reviewing one of the drafts and for her prompting to keep on to publication.

To Sheryl Guillaume for her great encouragement during my early days of writing and for reviewing one of my many drafts.

And to the staff at Friesen Press who have impressed me with their professional support and for getting me over that elusive finish line.

References

Chapter 2
Eckhart Tolle, *A New Earth,* Plume, 2006

Chapter 3
Wayne Dyer, *Manifest Your Destiny,* Harper Collins, 1997

Eckhart Tolle, *A New Earth,* Plume, 2006

Chapter 4
Stephen Covey, *The 7 Habits of Highly Effective People,* Free Press, 1989

Chapter 5
Eckhart Tolle, *The Power of Now,* Namaste Publishing, 1999

Chapter 7
Carolyn Myss, *Anatomy of the Spirit,* Three Rivers, 1996

Chapter 8
Eckhart Tolle, *The Power of Now*,
Namaste Publishing, 1999

Chapter 9
Neale Donald Walsch, *Conversations with God, Book One*, G.P. Putnam's Sons, 1995

Chapter 10
Jaqueline Bisset, in an interview after the Golden Globe awards

Isabelle Holland (quote could not be sourced)

Chapter 11
Neale Donald Walsch, *Conversations with God, Book Three*, G.P. Putnam's Sons, 1995

Chapter 12
Eckhart Tolle, *A New Earth*, Plume, 2006

Neale Donald Walsch, *Conversations with God, Book Three*, G.P. Putnam's Sons, 1995

Wayne Dyer, *The Power of Intention*, Hay House Inc., 2004

Leland Val Van DeWall, *Balanced Successful Living*, self-published course material, 1984

Neale Donald Walsch, *Conversations with God, Book One*, G.P. Putnam's Sons, 1995

Corrie ten Boom, *Clippings from my Notebook*, Thomas Nelson, Inc., 1982

Chapter 14
Viktor Frankl, *Man's Search for Meaning, Part One, Experiences in a Concentration Camp.* Pocket Books, 1959

CPSIA information can be obtained at www.ICGtesting.com
Printed in the USA
LVOW07s0525210116

470879LV00005B/38/P